Once in a Lifetime

Seizing Today's Opportunities for World Harvest

David Shibley

Sovereign World

Sovereign World
PO Box 777
Tonbridge
Kent TN11 0ZS
England

This Sovereign World book is distributed in North America by Renew Books, a ministry of Gospel Light, Ventura, California, USA. For a free catalog of resources from Renew Books/Gospel Light, please contact your Christian supplier or call 1-800-4-GOSPEL

ISBN: 1 85240 220 2

Typeset by CRB Associates, Reepham, Norfolk
Printed in England by Clays Ltd, St Ives plc.

About the Author

David Shibley is president and founder of Global Advance, a missions ministry providing training and tools for pastors and church leaders in developing nations. Global Advance has provided face-to-face training for over 100,000 church leaders, often in some of the neediest places on earth.

He is a graduate of John Brown University (where he was named Outstanding Alumnus of 1995) and Southwestern Baptist Theological Seminary. He also holds an honorary doctorate from Oral Roberts University. Having ministered in forty-eight nations, he is in demand as a speaker in missions conferences around the world and as an equipper of national church leaders. The author of thirteen books, he is also a speaker for the Promise Keepers men's conferences.

Because of his commitment to the cause of world evangelization, David Shibley serves on the boards of seven missions organizations as well as heading the ministry of Global Advance. He is recognized as a major voice for world missions and is the speaker on the nationally syndicated broadcast, *WorldWatch with David Shibley*.

David has been in ministry since 1966, when God called him as a teenager to preach the gospel. He and his wife, Naomi, have two grown sons.

For more information on Global Advance's ministry of training national church leaders, or for more information about the author's other publications and ministry products, please contact:

Global Advance
PO Box 742077
Dallas, Texas 75374–2077

Phone: 972–771–9042
Fax: 972–771–3315
E-mail: globaladv@earthlink.net

Contents

Chapter 1

Purpose
The Sweep of History

'The kingdom of the world has become the kingdom of our Lord and of his Christ, and he will reign for ever and ever.' (Revelation 11:15)

Ever since I was called to preach as a teenager I had dreamed of this night.

The prayer of many young people in the Western world who had been called of God throughout the Cold War years was, 'Lord, somehow, some way, **someday** let me preach the gospel in the Soviet Union!'

Atheistic communist ideology had kept the old Soviet Union and its eastern bloc allies essentially closed to Christian missions throughout my youth. But **suddenly**, as the 1990s dawned, the Holy Spirit orchestrated glorious, turbulent change. The Berlin Wall came crashing down. Joyful throngs filled the streets of Prague as the elixir of freedom brought new hope for the future. And the inconceivable happened – the 'Union of Soviet Socialist Republics' vanished from the face of the earth.

Since 1966 when I answered the call to preach I had

prayed for ministry opportunities in that region. Now, in a dramatic twist of history, they had come. There I was, standing in a side room in back of a stage in the Byelorussian city of Minsk, ready to walk on stage and proclaim the Good News!

But would anyone come to hear it?

I paced the floor of the little room and prayed, 'Lord, we've stepped out in faith and rented this auditorium that seats 1200 people.' (By the way, that's one of the few things the communists did right. They built beautiful concert halls in almost every city. Little did they realize they were building them for evangelistic crusades!) 'But, Lord, why would anyone be interested in hearing some preacher from Texas? All we've done is rent this hall and distribute a few flyers about the meetings. Lord, please put at least a few hundred people in those seats!'

I needn't have been so concerned. As I walked on stage I was dumbfounded at what I saw. Not only was every seat taken, hundreds more were standing around the walls. Guards had been posted at the entrance to the balcony; so many people had stuffed the balcony they feared it might collapse.

But the response was even more overwhelming. When I gave the invitation to receive Christ as Lord and Savior, hundreds of people literally ran to the front, eager, even desperate, for a new life in Jesus Christ.

That scene was repeated every night of the crusade. And when we offered copies of the Bible in Russian, it was the first time I had seen people actually crawl over each other to get their hands on a precious copy of the Scripture they had so long been denied.

God did not make a mistake when He chose **you** to bear Christ's name at this hinge of history between two millennia. He has intersected your life with a season of spectacular, even unparalleled, opportunity. This period of time is not unlike that which God described to His prophet.

> *'Look at the nations and watch – and be utterly amazed. For I am going to do something in your days that you would not believe, even if you were told.'*
>
> (Habakkuk 1:5)

Yet tragically, in the midst of stupendous global harvest, many Christians cannot put in the sickle and reap because they are in such a dense spiritual fog.

The Church's Identity Crisis

I have had the honor of ministering in almost 50 nations. The beauty of the body of Christ expressed through multiple cultures is indescribable. I have drunk deeply from the refreshing wells of the church's life in many nations.

So it is more than a little disturbing to discover that Christians in my own nation are by far the most introspective believers in all the world. We whine, 'I just want to know my purpose. I've got to reach my destiny!' We race all over the country going to 'Destiny Conferences' and devour tapes and books on 'Discovering Your Destiny.' It would be amusing if it were not so appalling. Even cloaking our self-centeredness in Christian garb and jargon cannot cover the nakedness of this 'cult of self' that is choking much of the Western church.

How can we ever hope to discover **our** purpose in the earth when we separate it from **God's** purposes in the earth? How will we ever know **our** destiny when we have so little identification with **God's** destiny for the nations?

It is certainly good to pray, 'Lord, what is Your will for my life?' But it is far better to pray, 'Lord, what is Your will for my **generation**? How do You want my life to fit into Your plan for my times?' Pursuing **God's purposes**, not ours, is the path to personal fulfillment.

Jesus wasn't kidding when He warned that those who would be self-protective in His kingdom are actually those most at risk.

> 'For whoever wants to save his life will lose it, but whoever loses his life for me and for the gospel will save it.'
> (Mark 8:35)

Today we talk in terms of self-fulfillment and self-actualization. Christians used to speak of self-sacrifice. Ironically, those who practiced self-sacrifice ended up a lot more self-fulfilled and self-actualized than today's Christians!

Why? Because they embraced the veracity of the Bible's clear teaching that one truly 'finds' his or her life only in laying it down for Christ and for the gospel.

It is time for all this pathetic navel-gazing in the Western church to stop! We must refocus off our purpose and on to God's purpose, off our own needs and on to the needs of others. William Booth, founder of the Salvation Army, was consumed with a passion for Jesus and a desire to lift others in His name. General Booth lived in a day of many inventions, including the telegraph. One day a wealthy philanthropist offered to telegraph one of Booth's sermons worldwide. Booth immediately accepted the offer.

'There is one stipulation,' the philanthropist cautioned. 'Your sermon can be only one word long.' General Booth was quick to comply. Here is Booth's masterpiece, his one-word sermon:

'**Others**.'

William Booth took seriously Paul's admonition in Philippians 2:4–11,

> *'Each of you should look not only to your own interests, but also to the interests of others. Your attitude should be the same as that of Christ Jesus: Who, being in very nature God, did not consider equality with God something to be grasped, but made himself nothing, taking the very nature of a servant, being made in human likeness. And being found in appearance as a man, he humbled himself and became obedient to death – even death on a cross! Therefore God exalted him to the highest place and gave him the name that is above every name, that at the name of Jesus ever knee should bow, in heaven and on earth and under the earth, and every tongue confess that Jesus Christ is Lord, to the glory of God the Father.'*

The church does not need to be bogged down (or fogged in) by an identity crisis. Nor do you. Our purpose is clear. The Great Commission could not be more lucid. As Thomas Coke, a founder of the world missions movement among Methodists observed, we are 'embarked on the most glorious and most important work in the world.'[1]

Romance at the Heart of the Universe

God's interest in redeeming humanity did not begin when Jesus issued the Great Commission to His followers to make disciples of all the nations. Actually, Jesus left the Great Commission as His last words on earth to underscore, not diminish, its importance. He was only reiterating what had always been the heartbeat of His Father, an aggressive compassion in dealing with humanity.

The natural consequence of Adam and Eve's rebellion was a desire to hide from God. But the Father-heart of God came calling. God employed an aggressive 'evangelistic' strategy as He lovingly forced our first parents to face their sin. From the moment humankind's fellowship with the Creator was broken, God has been in the business of restoring it.

As Christians, we believe in a linear view of history. History is headed in a very clear direction. The track has been laid and the train of God's purposes is moving toward a predetermined destination.

> '... the earth shall be full of the knowledge of the LORD
> As the waters cover the sea.'   (Isaiah 11:9 NKJV)

No government edict can thwart it, no embarrassment of the church's failure can stop it. **Jesus shall reign!**

Some years ago I was speaking at an interdenominational prayer rally in a Midwestern city in the United States. Somehow the press of that city thought the rally had partisan political undertones. It did not; we gathered merely as Christians across denominational lines to pray for harvest and revival. Nevertheless, when I arrived at the site of the rally, the press was there. 'Have you come to our city to make a political statement?' they queried.

'Yes, I have,' I responded.

Immediately they clicked on their tape recorders, the video cameras began to roll and the note pads and pens came out.

'Are you ready?' I smiled. 'Here's my political statement: **The kingdoms of this world will become the kingdoms of our Lord and of His Christ, and He will reign for ever and ever!** That's where I stand on the issue; that's my political statement!'

The Bible's integrating theme is the awesome story of how God Himself intervened to save His fallen creation that was bent on self-destruction. There is a scarlet thread of redemption clearly woven through all of Scripture. God's eternal purpose is to call out a bride for His Son from fallen humanity, thus receiving praise and glory for His marvelous grace. The composition of this radiantly beautiful, multi-ethnic bride will be redeemed people *'from every tribe and language and people and nation'* (Revelation 5:9).

As Paul Billheimer observed, 'There is romance at the heart of the universe.' Everything God is doing, He is doing for the purpose of creating a bride for His Son. And just as Abraham's 'no-name' servant was given the high dignity of finding a bride for Isaac, we have been commissioned to find a bride for our 'Isaac,' the Lord Jesus Christ. Our assignment is to cooperate with God by taking out from the nations *'a people for His name'* (Acts 15:14 NKJV). What a high purpose and honor!

God's Symphonic Crescendo

Two words from other languages help us understand something of the import of our times. The character for the word *crisis* in both the classical and simplified Chinese is composed of two smaller characters meaning 'danger' and 'opportunity.' Indeed, the crises of our times spell both danger and opportunity. Think of both the dangers and opportunities represented in mounting ethnic-based hostilities around the world, the worldwide epidemic of AIDS, curious viruses that are resistant to treatment, the disintegration of families, international drug gangs, political corruption, world hunger, blatant lawlessness, sexual promiscuity and increasing earthquakes and natural disasters. These global crises spell both danger and abundant opportunity for discerning Christians.

A biblical Greek word, *kairos*, describes a unique season of possibilities. By sovereign grace, God has chosen that your life be woven into 'the *kairos* hour' for world evangelization. When Scripture uses this word, it is usually in reference to a brief, specific season of God's favor. Using this word, Jesus refers to a *'time of harvest'* in Matthew 13:30 (NKJV) and Paul speaks of a *'due season'* for reaping in Galatians 6:9 (NKJV). And in such *kairos* seasons of opportunity, the Bible urges us to be *'redeeming the time'* (Ephesians 5:16 NKJV). One translation reads, 'Buy up the opportunities.'

This current era is a season the Bible would describe as the fullness of time. Throughout history God has made major transitions in His dealings with humanity in two thousand year increments. This leads many Christians to believe that extremely momentous events are poised to occur. As we race toward a new millennium, it is difficult to overstate the importance of the next few years for world evangelization.

For roughly two thousand years the church has been under mandate to disciple all nations. To put it bluntly, we have failed. But now, for the first time in two millennia, almost every major stream of Christianity is giving world evangelization top priority.

The Alpha course is rekindling evangelism in Britain's churches, from Anglican to Assemblies of God. The Pensacola awakening in the United States has swept tens of thousands into the kingdom and a deeper walk with God. Stadiums full of men ring out with strong praises to Jesus at Promise Keepers events. On every continent, with the possible exception of North America, the church is advancing.

Consider these exciting facts:

- During the twentieth century, Christianity has become the most extensive and universal religion in history.
- There are now more Christians in the Southern Hemisphere than in the Northern Hemisphere. The new centers of vitality for the church in many ways are in Africa, Asia and Latin America. This more than counterbalances the decline in the North Atlantic nations.
- Each day welcomes a net global increase of at least 176,000 Christians.
- Each week approximately one thousand new churches are planted in Asia and Africa alone.
- Christianity is now a genuinely international family of faith. Christianity has surged ahead in the world's less developed countries. From being predominately white, Christianity is now an amalgam of the races and peoples of the world, with whites dropping from more than 80 percent to about 35 percent.
- The proportion of Christians to the whole population will increase in Asia more than in any other region of the world.

Even secular authors like John Naisbitt in his book, *Megatrends 2000*, predict a simultaneous series of world-wide revivals. Consider the dramatic political changes like the integration of Hong Kong back into mainland China. Some call it 'crisis;' spiritually alert believers should see it as 'danger' **and** 'opportunity.'

Just as God demolished the formidable walls of Jericho, He is destroying walls of opposition today. This is why Dick Eastman, international president of Every Home for Christ, refers to this season as the 'Jericho hour' for world harvest. 'Recent miracles in once dark places globally give us cause for great hope,' Eastman writes. 'I truly believe this is the Jericho hour for the body of Christ. But we must capture the momentum of this season of suddenlies if our generation is to witness closure of the Great Commission.'[2]

As you read, I believe the Holy Spirit is stirring you. He prods you today, much as Mordecai did when he asked his niece, Queen Esther,

> *'Who knows whether you have come to the kingdom for such a time as this?'* (Esther 4:14 NKJV)

The breakup of the old Soviet Union and the opening of the eastern bloc nations to the gospel at the beginning of the 1990s was something of a trial balloon the Holy Spirit was sending up. He was saying to us, 'What will you do with mega-opportunities? Will you be a righteous steward of this *kairos* season? Will you finally seize your destiny and align your life's purpose with the purposes of God in your generation?

Now the compelling question comes to you: **So what?**

What will **you do** in light of the hour God has placed you in history?

Do you have a sense of stewardship of these fantastic opportunities?

Will you live with some sense of appreciation of these seasonal challenges for the gospel's global advance?

Will you pray, think and strategize globally?

Will you live for eternity, realizing that at the Judgment Seat of Christ you must 'give an account of your stewardship' in these momentous days?

Or, when you stand before the Lord, will you try to sputter out a reason for being spiritually comatose, 'business as usual,' through the most hope-filled hour of harvest in two thousand years?

As one looks at the colossal needs and even more colossal opportunities, one wants to cry out with

Jeremiah, *'Is it nothing to you, all you who pass by?'* (Lamentations 1:12).

Well ... is it?

Does it make any difference to you? Will anyone be in heaven who would not otherwise have been there because you faced these questions today? Will this confrontation result in transformation ... in you? In nations?

If not, why don't you spare yourself the effort and stop reading now.

God's Purpose and Yours

World missions was woven into the fabric of my Christian upbringing. So the self-serving teachings of some, suggesting that we should heap blessings on ourselves instead of a needy world, sound shrill to my ears. In my family's framework of faith, all we had was for the benefit of those who didn't have. With the apostle Paul, we sensed an acute debt to bring the gospel and its attendant blessings to our generation.

God has put us here for a purpose. We are people of destiny. God has raised up this generation of Christian believers to be a force in the earth. And we are living now in a season of spectacular missions opportunity that comes only once in a lifetime.

Since Jesus issued His Great Commission, the church's purpose has always been pristine and clear. **The purpose of the church is to bring God glory through the worldwide proclamation, reception and worship of His Son**. This is our corporate purpose. It should be our individual purpose as well.

The Westminster Shorter Catechism asks, 'What is the sole purpose of man?' The answer is simple, profound and biblical: 'The sole purpose of man is to glorify God and to enjoy Him forever.'

How, then, do we glorify God? We glorify Him by obedience to His directives, drawing on the power of His life in us. In other words, the most God-honoring, purpose-satisfying, destiny-fulfilling life is a life controlled by the Holy Spirit and fully submissive to His promptings and clear commands.

We are in the final minutes of this millennium. This is the *kairos* season for world harvest. It is also clearly a late hour in God's prophetic timetable. It is too late to be little; too near the end to be frivolous. With our purpose clearly set, we go to make a difference in our perilous world.

References

1. Cyril Davey, *Mad About Mission*, Basingstoke, Hants: Marshall Pickering, 1985, p. 115.
2. Dick Eastman, *The Jericho Hour*, Lake Mary, Fla.: Creation House, 1994, p. 21.

Chapter 2

Peril
Without God, Without Hope

'[God] *will punish those who do not know God and do not obey the gospel of our Lord Jesus. They will be punished with everlasting destruction and shut out from the presence of the Lord and from the majesty of his power.*'

(2 Thessalonians 1:8, 9)

I could not speak for hours.

The tour of the death camps at Auschwitz and walking through the hermetically sealed 'shower room' where thousands were suffocated with deadly Zyklon-B gas left me nauseated and smitten by our sinful condition. Man's inhumanity to man overwhelmed me. Humanity's shame still hung heavy over the place, even fifty years after its atrocities. I thought of the words of poet Robert Browning, 'There may be a heaven, but there must be a hell.'

Lest we think the Nazi perpetrators of this despicable evil are somehow 'different than us,' let's remember the muted almost non-existent protest of the world community against the same level of cruelty in Bosnia, Burundi and Sudan. Surely Jews, understanding the horrors of the holocaust, would raise their voices against the death camps in Bosnia. But they did not. (Perhaps because most of the victims were Muslims.) Surely Christians would protest the blasphemous crucifixions of fellow Christians in Sudan. But listen again to our guilty silence.

Are we ashamed that humanity's sworn promise to 'never again' witness another holocaust has been shattered in less than fifty years? Do we somehow intrinsically know that, outside of the lift of regeneration, we are all capable of the most horrific acts? Is there not an innate cry for justice and an equal cry that we are incapable of effecting justice in our fallen world? Do we not hope against hope that there is a coming day when a holy God will execute both matchless grace and perfect judgment?

Eternal matters often seem irrelevant to a generation baptized in hedonism and existentialism. Yet, in the deep recesses of our hearts, we know we must face the issue. 'Hell is the most offensive and least acceptable of all Christian doctrines,' writes David Pawson. 'We try to ignore it but it won't go away. We attempt to explain it away but it keeps coming back. Better to face the truth, even if it hurts.' Pawson further asserts, 'I am convinced that the recovery of this neglected truth is vital to the health of Christ's body and essential to the task of completing the evangelization of all the nations.'[1] I share David Pawson's conviction in this regard.

Too often we major in minors while minoring in majors. Christian missions is based on several givens – assumptions on which the passion for global evangelism rests. One of the most basic of these assumptions is that people who are without Jesus Christ are lost. I firmly believe that one's emotional involvement in missions will be in direct proportion to the strength of one's belief in the doctrine of the lostness of mankind. This evangelistic passion gripped John Wesley.

> 'Whenever I see one or a thousand men running into hell, be it in England, Ireland, or France, yea, in Europe, Asia, Africa or America, I will stop them if I can. As a minister of Christ, I will beseech them in His name, to turn back and be reconciled to God.'

Jesus spoke far more often of hell than He did of heaven. Our Lord said,

> *'Wide is the gate and broad is the road that leads to destruction, and many enter through it.'*
>
> (Matthew 7:14)

The Greek word for 'destruction' is *apoleia*, clearly a reference to eternal perdition. The eminent theologian and church father, Augustine, concurred. 'Our friends who long to get rid of eternal punishment should cease to argue against God and instead obey God's commands while there is still time.'

While most evangelicals would still give doctrinal consent to eternal punishment, often we do not emotionally come to grips with its consequences. If people are lost outside of Christ, and if faith in Jesus Christ is the only avenue of redemption, what could possibly be a higher priority than spreading the gospel as far as we can as fast as we can? Anything the church does that is not directly tied to evangelism is not unlike rearranging the furniture while the house is on fire!

In my opinion, no theological issue could be more crucial for evangelism and missions than how deeply we really believe that people without Christ are eternally lost and that there is salvation in no one else. There is no other name given that can redeem them (see Acts 4:12). This is **the** watershed theological issue for evangelicals as we enter the twenty-first century.

I fully agree with those who say that the **highest** motive for world evangelization is the honor of Jesus Christ, not the threat of eternal punishment for unbelievers. I am quick to admit that an inspiration to 'evangelize the heathen' has sometimes led to simplistic methods and gravely embarrassing cultural mistakes in missions history. Nevertheless, David Pawson is right when he states that 'missionary strategists who consider that a more mature approach can do without such inspiration have yet to prove that this stimulates greater, or even equal, zeal.'[2]

Is Humanity Really Lost?

The story is told that Charlie Peace, a convicted murderer, took one parting shot at a complacent church in a conversation with the chaplain in Leeds prison, before he was hanged.

> 'Sir, if I believed what you and the church of God say you believe, even if England were covered in broken glass from coast to coast, I would walk over it, if need be on my hands and knees, and think it worthwhile living just to save one soul from an eternal hell like that.'[3]

Surely the urgency of our witness will measure the reality of our beliefs.

Even in theologically conservative circles, we are battling a new, creeping universalism. Some who are otherwise

Bible-believing Christians seem to cringe at the reality of judgment, especially for those who have never heard the gospel. It is not that they have formally removed their belief in hell and judgment. There is simply an eerie silence, even among evangelicals, as many endeavor to sort out in their hearts what they hold to be true.

While a true evangelical could never embrace pure universalism, some are embracing annihilationism, the teaching that unbelievers are eventually simply annihilated rather than suffering everlasting judgment. I have the utmost respect for John Stott as a careful theologian and conscientious Christian. Nevertheless, it was grievous to me to see this prime architect of the magnificent Lausanne Covenant make a 'tentative suggestion' that 'eternal punishment may mean the ultimate annihilation of the wicked rather than their eternal conscious torment.'[4]

Will some evangelicals' endorsement of annihilationism lead eventually to an endorsement of universalism? We do not know. What we do know is that universalism, the belief that all people will eventually be saved, is never a friend to evangelism and missions. Billy Graham has said,

> 'The various shades of universalism prevalent throughout the church have done more to blunt evangelism and take the heart out of the missionary movement than anything else. I believe the Scriptures teach that men outside of Jesus Christ are lost.'[5]

It should be underscored, however, that the character of God is not on trial. Our belief in the Bible is on trial but God's justice is not. The God of all the earth will do right. Any decision He makes regarding those who have not heard will be executed according to His standards of equally perfect righteousness and love.

Nevertheless, neither Scripture nor the church's historic posture is unclear as to the final destiny of those without Christ. Scripture clearly describes a coming apocalypse:

> '... *when the Lord Jesus is revealed from heaven in blazing fire with his powerful angels. He will punish those who do not know God and do not obey the gospel of our Lord Jesus. They will be punished with everlasting destruction and shut out from the presence of the Lord and from the majesty of his power.*'
>
> (2 Thessalonians 1:7–9)

Polycarp, one of the early church fathers, faced a vicious martyrdom in a Roman arena with wild beasts. The proconsul urged the aged Christian to renounce his faith in Christ but to no avail. Finally the authority threatened, 'I will have you consumed with fire, if you despise wild beasts, unless you change your mind.'

Polycarp replied, 'You threaten with fire which burns for an hour and is soon quenched; for you are ignorant of the fire of the coming judgement and eternal punishment reserved for the wicked.' Polycarp, having already given himself up for dead, sought only the salvation of his executioner.[6]

To the testimony of the Scriptures and countless Christian martyrs, the historic creeds of the church add their affirmation of a real heaven and a real hell. One of the great theological documents of history is the Westminster Confession. This statement of faith uniformly declares,

> 'But the wicked, who know not God, and obey not the gospel of Jesus Christ, shall be cast into eternal torments, and be punished with everlasting

destruction from the presence of the Lord and the glory of His power.'

In more recent times as well, evangelical Christians have affirmed the reality not only of a place of eternal blessing but also a place of eternal torment. The Baptist Faith and Message states,

> 'The unrighteous will be consigned to Hell, the place of everlasting punishment. The righteous, in their resurrected and glorified bodies, will receive their reward and will dwell forever in Heaven with the Lord.'

The Statement of Fundamental Truths of the Assemblies of God declares,

> 'Whosoever is not found written in the Book of Life, together with the devil and his angels, the beast, and the false prophet, will be consigned to everlasting punishment in the lake which burneth with fire and brimstone, which is the second death.'

The most often quoted verse in the Bible clearly presents humanity's only two options: perishing or having everlasting life.

> *'For God so loved the world that he gave his one and only Son, that whoever believes in him shall not perish but have eternal life.'* (John 3:16)

The subsequent verses remind us that God's disposition toward humankind is love and forgiveness:

> *'For God did not send his Son into the world to condemn the world, but to save the world through him. Whoever*

believes in him is not condemned, but whoever does not believe stands condemned already because he has not believed in the name of God's one and only Son ... Whoever believes in the Son has eternal life, but whoever rejects the Son will not see life, for God's wrath remains on him.' (John 3:17, 18, 36)

Those outside of Christ live in constant peril because they are under God's judgment.

As Paul thought of his own people being lost, he wrote,

'I have great sorrow and unceasing anguish in my heart.' (Romans 9:2)

He added that he would be willing to give up his place in Christ and be separated from Him if by such a sacrifice others would be saved. Paul believed all people outside of Christ were lost, and it left him with a broken heart.

It is precisely this scandal of an unbroken heart that impedes evangelism today. We need a fresh baptism of the kind of compassion that led William Booth to suggest that if he could, he would include fifteen minutes in hell in the training of all Salvation Army officers. He knew that would keep their priorities right and prepare them for a life of urgent, compassionate ministry.

Are there any left today who weep instead of sleep, agonizing before God for the lost? Glorious harvest is promised to those who have sown in tears.

'Those who sow in tears
  will reap with songs of joy.
He who goes out weeping,
  carrying seed to sow,
will return with songs of joy,
  carrying sheaves with him.' (Psalm 126:5–6)

The crown of rejoicing awaits those who win souls (see 1 Thessalonians 2:19–20).

> *'Those who are wise will shine like the brightness of the heavens, and those who lead many to righteousness, like the stars for ever and ever.'* (Daniel 12:3)

Jesus Christ is truth incarnate. Truth cannot utter an untruth. He clearly declared, *'No one comes to the Father except through me'* (John 14:6). Jesus spoke often of the terrible place of torment for those who were not reconciled to God. He told the story of an arrogant, wealthy man who, in hell, screamed and pleaded for just a drop of water. The man cried, *'I am in agony in this fire'* (Luke 16:24). Jesus said there would be those who would go *'into the eternal fire'* (Matthew 25:41) and *'to eternal punishment'* (Matthew 25:46).

Jesus came from heaven to earth on a rescue mission. God is not desirous that anyone perish (see 2 Peter 3:9). We should share the heart of God. Jesus tasted death for every person (see Hebrews 2:9). That means the potential of redemption stretches to the entire human race. Look again at Calvary. See God's Son as He hangs on the cross. In history's most awesome moment, He who knew no sin became sin for us (2 Corinthians 5:21). Your sins, my sins, the sins of the entire world were in that moment smashed on Him. The literal meaning of Isaiah 53:6 is, *'...the Lord has caused to land on Him the iniquity of us all.'* Jesus Christ was separated from the Father so that we might never need to be separated from Him.

What if They Haven't Heard?

A young person came to me some time ago with a troubled look on his face. 'I love the Lord and I believe the Bible,' he told me. 'But I just can't believe that God would condemn someone who has never heard the gospel.' Let's face squarely this difficult question. What if they haven't heard?

In the first chapter of Romans Paul makes an excellent case for the lostness of humanity. He reminds us that men and women are not only going to be lost when they die – they are born in sin as descendants of Adam and inherently separated from God. The Bible says the un-believing person *'stands condemned already'* and that *'God's wrath remains on him'* (John 3:18, 36). Paul gives an airtight argument that every person stands account-able to God because of the light of conscience and the testimony of God in creation.

This testimony of nature is sometimes called general revelation. Creation's general revelation of God power-fully preaches a person's accountability to his or her Creator. However, only the specific revelation of God in Jesus Christ shows how we can be justified before this holy Creator-God. According to Paul, even the remotest of peoples are 'without excuse' because of the light of conscience and nature. Yet only the light of the world, Jesus Christ, can bring them salvation.

It is important to understand that rejection of the gospel is not the only criterion for lostness. Humanity is already lost because of sin. That blankets all people everywhere.

'For all have sinned and fall short of the glory of God.'
(Romans 3:23)

We are sinners because of the wrongs we have done. But we are also sinners because of who we are – children of Adam. As his offspring, we are born with a proclivity to sin. Humanity is already in darkness.

A word of warning needs to be added here. Those of us

who live in nations historically blessed with the gospel have had the privilege of a much brighter light. Individual Christians, churches and media have drenched my country with the Good News. God's Word makes clear that the greater the light rejected, the greater the condemnation. I believe the Bible teaches that many so-called 'Christian nations' will face a judgment stiffer than that of other nations.

> *'How much more severely do you think a man deserves to be punished who has trampled the Son of God under foot, who has treated as an unholy thing the blood of the covenant that sanctified him, and who has insulted the Spirit of grace?'*   (Hebrews 10:29)

When those from my country stand before God the question will not be, 'What about the people who haven't heard?' The question will be, 'What about you? You **have** heard.'

Again it needs to be stated that God's character is not on trial. He can be trusted to do what is completely just and right. When we ponder His mercy, this whole issue is flipped. Since God is perfectly holy, the wonder is not that some will be lost. The great wonder is that anyone from rebellious humanity is saved! Only Christ's work on the cross could reconcile us to God.

God has gone to the very limits of boundless love to prevent humankind from perishing. God incarnate became sin incarnate on the cross! It is much too much to fathom fully. Yet it is wonderfully true. As we moved toward judgment, God intervened personally through Christ.

> *'He is the atoning sacrifice for our sins, and not only for ours but also for the sins of the whole world.'*
>   (1 John 2:2)

The question of the lostness of those who have not heard the gospel is a vital issue. It must be resolved in one's heart (at least by faith) before missionary passion can flow in fullness. While the question is usually raised in sincerity, the one who doubts the lostness of those who haven't heard should carry that argument to its logical conclusion. If those who haven't heard are not accountable, we should immediately rush every missionary home and prevent every national worker from reaching any further. After all, what if those previously unaccountable were to hear the gospel and reject it? They would then be accountable. The missionary would have done them a terrible disservice. Such a line of reasoning would have to conclude that the kindest thing we could do for yet unreached humanity would be to stop preaching the gospel! It is little wonder that such reasoning dwarfs missionary advance.

But in fact those who have not heard the gospel are just as lost as those who have heard and rejected it. Therefore, the most benevolent, humanitarian activity in the world is preaching the gospel. The benefits of reception of the message begin immediately. Time and again, social transformation has resulted from the infiltration of the gospel into society. But the benefits are also eternal.

The sincerity of most of the adherents of the world's great religions is not in question. Yet sincerity is not what saves us. Only faith in the finished work of Jesus Christ brings salvation. Holy Scripture does not suggest any alternative plan. We have a distinct message – the only message that can set humanity's captives free. As someone has said, 'The gospel is not a message that we would invent if we could nor one we could invent if we would.' The Christian message does not parrot other religions. Our faith is gloriously unique.

'We Have to Go Out'

In light of Christ's sacrifice, we must go, endued with the
Spirit's power to actualize that for which Christ died. It
was this motivation that spurred Nikolaus von Zinzendorf and the Moravian missionaries 'to win for the Lamb
the reward of His sacrifice.' Paul, that great missionary,
cried, *'I am compelled to preach. Woe to me if I do not preach
the gospel!'* (1 Corinthians 9:16). John Knox pleaded on
his knees, 'Give me Scotland or I die.' As a young man
Hudson Taylor cried out to God, 'I feel that I cannot go
on living unless I do something for China.' Robert
Arthington could not go overseas but, through sacrifice,
helped send others. He lived in a single room, cooked his
own meals and gave over half a million dollars to
missions. At the end of his life he wrote, 'Gladly would I
again make the floor my bed, a box my chair, another
box my table, rather than that men should perish for
want of the knowledge of the Savior.' As Amy Carmichael
left Britain for India, never to return to her native land,
she said, 'There is nothing too precious for Jesus.'

Each of these persons had a heart pumping with what
Oswald J. Smith called a 'passion for souls.' Do you
have that passion? Do you long for more? The believer
who is intimate with the Holy Spirit is advantaged here.
Why?

> *'Because God has poured out his love into our hearts by
> the Holy Spirit.'* (Romans 5:5)

Late one night a concerned lighthouse keeper watched
from the tower as a violent storm erupted at sea.
Suddenly the seasoned keeper saw the faint signal of a
ship in distress, pleading for help. Instinctively he turned
to his young apprentice and commanded, 'Let's go!'

Horrified, the apprentice retorted, 'But, sir, if we go out there, we may never come back.'

The old keeper of the lighthouse paused and put his hand on the young man's shoulder. 'Son,' he responded, 'we have to go out. We don't have to come back.'

No one doubts that there is a great peril in penetrating the final frontiers. But that is not the issue. What matters is that people are perishing. We have to go out. We don't have to come back. The global Christian advance is a rescue operation. The mercy of God is extended toward humanity. This is the day of God's grace, the hour of our greatest opportunity. So it's time to talk about priorities.

References

1. David Pawson, *The Road to Hell*, London: Hodder & Stoughton, 1992.
2. *Ibid.*, p. 77.
3. *Ibid.*, p. v.
4. Roy McCloughry, 'Basic Stott: Candid comments on Justice, Gender and Judgment,' *Christianity Today*, January 8, 1996, p. 18.
5. Arthur Johnstone, *The Battle for World Evangelism*, Wheaton, Ill.: Tyndale House, 1978, p. 168.
6. John Braun, *Whatever Happened to Hell?* Nashville, Tenn.: Thomas Nelson, 1979, pp. 105–106.

Chapter 3

Priority
The Day of Visitation

'Take your sickle and reap, because the time to reap has come, for the harvest of the earth is ripe.' (Revelation 14:15)

I stood on Brighton Beach and drank in the crisp sea breeze as it washed across my face. It was summer, 1992. As I looked out toward the European continent I thought back to a very different time but the same place.

It was the same scene, Brighton Beach, but the year was 1850. Hudson Taylor, still a teenager and only recently converted, surrendered his life to God for China on this wind-swept sandy beach. In the aftermath of that experience with God at Brighton, Taylor said, 'I feel that I cannot go on living unless I do something for China.' Hudson Taylor sailed for China in 1853 and later founded the China Inland Mission.

The ramifications of that commitment at Brighton are still being felt in China today. In fact, Ruth Tucker asserts that 'no other missionary in the nineteen centuries since the apostle Paul has had a wider vision and has carried out a more systematized plan of evangelizing a broad geographical area than Hudson Taylor.'[1]

As the salt water sprayed my face I prayed, 'God, do it again.'

The Cain Mentality

Hudson Taylor's life priority was to bring the gospel and its social lift and blessings to the people of China. He was clearly focused on fulfilling Christ's Great Commission in the vast reaches of China's inland. As he matured in his walk with the Lord, Taylor would discover what he termed 'the exchanged life,' as he learned to rely on the dynamism of the indwelling Christ rather than human strength to get the job done.

As with Paul before him, once he met Jesus Christ, Hudson Taylor's priorities were radically changed. Along with Paul, he felt that he was a debtor to bring the gospel to those who had not heard it. And with Paul he pursued the vision with a whole-hearted passion. Paul wrote:

> *'I am obligated both to Greeks and non-Greeks, both to the wise and the foolish. That is why I am so eager to preach the gospel also to you who are at Rome.'*
>
> (Romans 1:14, 15)

But this kind of language, much less this kind of passion, is extraneous to many Christians today. To be sure, we continue to speak of **vision**, but we no longer speak of **burden**. We hear much about **destiny** but almost nothing about **dying to self**. We exult in **the joy of the Lord** but **travail for souls** is foreign to us. Such agonizing for the lost might even be viewed by some as a 'lack of faith.' This generation of Christians speaks of **self-fulfillment** and **self-actualization**. Taylor's generation of believers understood **self-sacrifice**.

Look at the shift of focus. No longer is the object God or even others. The new center of attraction is self! We have lost a sense of accountability for the lost condition of humanity.

Once after I preached on our missions responsibility, an obviously irritated woman approached me. 'What does that have to do with me?' she snapped. 'What do needy children in Africa have to do with my needs? Who made me accountable?'

She had cornered herself with her own questions. Who indeed has made us accountable? Our Lord and God. I do not wish to be unkind. Nevertheless, I admit that priority number one for too many of us is not the glory of God but the blessing of ourselves. Some have been infested with a 'Cain mentality.' The Cain mentality quips, 'Am I my brother's keeper? Who made me accountable?'

The Jesus heart responds, 'My nourishment is to do the will of the Father and to finish His work.' We must resonate Paul's heartbeat. We **are** obligated to those without the gospel. And in this, our once in a lifetime opportunity, we must pull out all the stops so that we too are 'eager to preach the gospel.'

Any church that is not seriously involved in world evangelization has forfeited its biblical right to exist! Any Christian who just flatly doesn't care whether or not people crash into eternity without God does violence to the heart of the gospel and the heart of Jesus. Such a Christian is a walking paradox, no matter how orthodox his or her theology may be.

The Jonah Mentality

Yet many Christians are completely unmoved by the fate of the unconverted and wholly disinterested in the purposes of God in their generation. The same Christians who yawn with boredom when **missions** is mentioned are often impassioned in their denunciations against society's sins.

Hey, don't we get it? Lost people are just acting – lost! Unsaved people are just acting – unsaved! If we **really** want to see the social order redeemed and morality restored, we'd better get back into seeing **people** redeemed and restored!

But maybe there's something far more sinister at work here. Perhaps **our** hearts need to be changed every bit as much as the hearts of the unconverted. Too many of us are just like Jonah; we don't **want** to see the unrighteous find mercy. We enjoy thundering God's judgment but the prospect that pimps, terrorists and homosexuals might actually repent and find forgiveness sends us into a psychological tailspin, just as it did Jonah. In fact, Jonah was so 'depressed' over God's kindness, he wanted God to take his life!

After Jonah had trumpeted his prophetic warning to debauched Nineveh the city came clean before God with heart-felt repentance. But was Jonah pleased that God's mercy had overridden His judgment? Hardly! 'I knew that you are a gracious and compassionate God,' Jonah whined. 'I knew you would be slow to anger and abounding in love toward these perverts. I knew you would relent from sending calamity on these swine! Just what kind of God **are** you, anyway?'

Good question. Here's a small part of the answer. Unlike the Hindu gods, He is perfect and only one omnipotent God suffices for every human cry for divine intervention. Unlike the Muslim concept of Allah, God goes far beyond mercy to bestow grace and relationship to undeserving sinners. Unlike the concept that even some Christians have of God, because of the cross of

Christ, God's first disposition toward humanity is love, not judgment.

And lest we forget, it's because God **is** 'gracious, compassionate, slow to anger, abounding in love' that we ever got into His family!

One of America's outstanding pastors shared with me how his 'righteous indignation' almost short-circuited one of the greatest sweeps of God's Spirit in our lifetime. The year was 1969 and hippies everywhere were challenging the status quo. My pastor friend had allowed his youth pastor to open a coffee house to minister to these kids, although he wanted no part of it himself.

The youth pastor befriended these counter-culture kids and showed real concern for them. As a result, one unforgettable Sunday evening, thirty hippies marched down to the front rows of the church and took their seats. The conservative church sat in dumbfounded, judgmental silence as long-haired boys in sandals shuffled down the aisles with their arms around girls in halter tops and cut-off jeans.

My pastor friend decided it was time to take action. 'I was one sentence away from telling our ushers to escort these hippies out of the building for being disrespectful to God's house,' he told me. 'But then the Holy Spirit arrested me.'

'What's the title of your message tonight?' the Holy Spirit tapped at his heart.

'Christ is the Answer,' he replied.

'Well,' the Spirit prodded, 'is He the answer for **them**?'

Broken before the Lord, my friend repented and lovingly delivered the gospel. Almost every one of those young people opened their hearts that night to Christ.

That was the beginning of a revival that would see over 1500 teenagers swept into the kingdom through that one church. Out of the revival that began that night, early contemporary Christian music received some of its finest talent. Petra, Nancy Honeytree and Jeoffrey Benward all came to Christ in that awakening.

And it was one sentence away from being aborted.

Now, what about you? Who are you judging? Who do you write off as past redemption? Look at those Christians often despise. What about the Iraqi soldiers who shot the scuds at Tel Aviv? What about the Muslim terrorists who blew up the marine barracks in Saudi Arabia? What about the heartless communist officials who harass and sometimes 'neutralize' Christians in China, just for attending an 'unregistered' church?' What about the Christ-haters who literally crucify Christians in Sudan?

What if **they** started asking forgiveness and professing faith in Jesus? What if the child molesters and drug addicts say they'd like to come to your church, just as inquirers? Would you receive them? Or would you usher them out?

A lack of compassion left Jonah spiritually, mentally and emotionally imbalanced. He became a lot more concerned about a vine providing shade for him than he was for the fate of thousands of people. While we might view Jonah's actions as somewhat deranged, they are a perfect picture of too many Christians who are far more concerned with their own shade and shelter than the impending doom of the city.

Baptism of Compassion

Yet God is more than willing to give us a fresh baptism of compassion. He wants to perform 'eye surgery' on us so we can bring things back into proper focus. Are you willing for such a surgery?

If you're willing, I challenge you to pray two dangerous

prayers. First, **ask the Holy Spirit to pour out God's love into your heart**. The Bible says,

> *'God has poured out his love into our hearts by the Holy Spirit, whom he has given us.'*　　　　(Romans 5:5)

Let God wash away the anger and bitterness, replacing it with His love. After all, love is the most potent weapon in the Christian's arsenal. You can counter words with words. You can counter rhetoric with rhetoric. You can counter bombs with bombs. But aggressive love – how do you counter **that**?

Second, **ask God for the gift of tears**. How lacking this is today. Yet the Bible says,

> *'Those who sow in tears*
> *　　will reap with songs of joy.*
> *He who goes out weeping,*
> *　　carrying seed to sow,*
> *will return with songs of joy,*
> *　　carrying sheaves with him.'*　　(Psalm 126:5, 6)

God has given us precious seed, the seed of the gospel. May He grace us to water that seed with tears.

I am not suggesting that we become emotional basket cases. But perhaps the truly emotionally imbalanced are not the sensitive but the **insensitive**. Some Christians seem to see tears as incompatible with victorious, faith-filled living. Yet those who weep are in good company.

> *'Jesus wept.'*　　　　(John 11:35)

When conditions warrant it, we ought to weep. Daily I pray that I will not go through these last days of the twentieth century in some kind of spiritual stupor, drugged by entertainment or indifference and thus unresponsive to humanity's agonies.

Before you read this next paragraph, ask the Holy Spirit to prepare your heart:

'While in my study one Sunday afternoon preparing to speak on the vastness of world harvest, I was suddenly overwhelmed by the sheer numbers of unsaved human beings. Quickly calculating a total of 5.384 billion inhabitants on earth, with only 1.5 billion of them even professing Christianity, I arrived at a minimum of 3.884 billion individuals alive on planet earth today who are on their way to an eternity without God. Allowing one foot per person in a single file line and compressing the line so tightly that not even a piece of paper could fit between the individuals, I pictured the line beginning in front on the pulpit of our sanctuary in Baton Rouge, Louisiana. To my amazement, my calculations showed it stretched east to the coast of Georgia and over the entire Atlantic ocean. Crossing Europe, spanning all of Russia and China, it even bridged the vast Pacific and touched California before re-entering our church sanctuary in the western entrance. It made an entire revolution around the earth! My heart beating faster with discovery, I continued my calculation to discover the line circling the globe twice ... four times ... eight times. I was almost in tears with compassion as I continued circling the globe with line after line of the eternally lost ... **twenty-five lines around.**' [2]

I read those lines to a friend one day as we sat in my car. As I read, tears glistened in his eyes. By the time I was finished, he was sobbing, pouring out his heart to God in behalf of the billions in our world in need of Jesus Christ. Is it any wonder that this friend is also one of the best witnesses for Christ I know? Are you surprised to know that he heads a worldwide missions organization that sees thousands come to Christ each year and has been responsible for planting hundreds of new churches?

The Day of Visitation

Do you remember that dramatic scene when Jesus stood outside the city of Jerusalem and wept over its impending destruction? Jesus was literally moved to tears *'because you did not know the time of your visitation'* (Luke 19:44 NKJV).

This is God's hour of visitation for global spiritual harvest. God has sovereignly ordained that this generation of believers have within its grasp what earlier generations of Christians could only dream of – closure on the Great Commission. We must be honorable stewards of this precious gift of a global visitation of God's Spirit for harvest.

I live and work every day on three premises. First, because I am a part of the renewal of God's Spirit in the church, I bear a heightened responsibility to evangelize the world. I espouse the present-day working of the Holy Spirit, complete with the possibility for all of the manifestations of His gifts. Since I endorse miracles and faith up front, this heightens my responsibility to be a world Christian.

Second, because I am a part of the church in the affluent Western world, I bear a heightened responsibility for world evangelization. While the power of the global church has shifted to the church in less developed nations, the Western church still bears heightened responsibility for world harvest because of our affluence and influence. Most of the Bible schools and Christian

41

publishing houses are in the Western world. Churches with the largest budgets are in the Western world.[3] This only augments our global accountability.

Third, because more people are receptive to the gospel than ever in history, this too augments our responsibility to give world evangelization top priority. **The Holy Spirit has orchestrated the events of this planet to indicate that world evangelization must be our top priority for the remainder of this century**. What part has God ordained for Spirit-renewed Christians to play in the global harvest? Why have we been entrusted with heaven's power? What about the large churches that sprouted in the 1980s? Were they birthed simply to bless their own constituents? What about the renewal in many churches in Britain and America in the 1990s? Was God's ultimate purpose merely to show people that they could be happy in church? Or does God have some bigger, more noble design?

Mordecai reminded his niece, Queen Esther, that she had been brought to the kingdom *'for such a time as this.'* God had sovereignly intersected Esther's life with a one-chance, go-for-broke, win-it-all-or-lose-it-all situation. Just so, God has sovereignly orchestrated events to mesh a worldwide renewal with a once in a lifetime opportunity. By sovereign grace, it has fallen on our generation to have within our grasp that for which other generations of Christians could only dream – closure on world evangelization.

If not us, who? If not now, when? If it is not this generation of Christians – we who have seen God's gracious renewal, we who possess more data on global harvest than any previous generation, we who stand on the shoulders of twenty centuries of missionary giants – if it is not us God wants to use to evangelize the world, then **who else** is it?

And if we are not to throw all our hearts and energies into the global harvest now – as the Spirit sweeps from nation to nation, now that we have actually isolated the remaining 1,739 unreached peoples, now as eschatological hopes are escalated as we face a new millennium – then, **when** will there be a more opportune time?

I am not suggesting that we run off in all directions, merely with human energy that is fueled by a noble cause. I **am** urging that we be imbued with the spirit of the sons of Issachar *'who understood the times and knew what Israel should do'* (1 Chronicles 12:32). May we too have an understanding of our times to lead God's people in what they should do. This is no time to be idle, it's a time to work long hours by the Spirit's empowering in the Father's ripe vineyard. As we work, let's remember that harvest is seasonal. Urgency should press us on. Jesus said,

> *'As long as it is day, we must do the work of him who sent me. Night is coming, when no one can work.'*
>
> (John 9:4)

God's Spirit is ever pointing in one direction – toward the preeminence of Jesus Christ. And He is ever pressing us toward one great goal – the fulfilling of the Great Commission. For the first time since the first century, the evangelization of the world is within our grasp. Events many thought impossible just a few years ago are now exploding all around us. Evangelical Christians are growing at four times the rate of population growth in Latin America. The *Four Spiritual Laws* are being passed out in Russian high schools. The percentage of Christians in India has soared in the 1990s from less than three percent to perhaps as high as eight percent. There is rapid church growth in the midst of and perhaps because of persecution of believers in China and the Muslim world. Surely we have been brought to the kingdom for such a time as this.

Light or Blight?

There will never be a better time to finish the job. We must hear and obey the Spirit's injunction to put in the sickle and reap now, before night falls. Without sounding melodramatic, it could be argued that, if we fail, the church could plunge into a second 'dark ages.' When we look at the immensity of the task, our hearts cry, 'Lord, who is sufficient for these things?' Yet we remember that nothing, including the evangelization of the world, is too hard for God.

> *'But we have this treasure in jars of clay to show that this all-surpassing power is from God and not from us.'*
>
> (2 Corinthians 4:7)

As we petition the Lord of the harvest, we can be confident that He will thrust out laborers and that a glorious harvest will be the result. In the late 1960s, Dick Eastman took a group of California teenagers on a weekend prayer retreat. A spirit of travail and intercession for their friends took hold of those young people. As they agonized before God for the souls of their generation, God met them in a powerful way, assuring them that He would answer dramatically. Within just a few months the Jesus Movement was sweeping thousands of California's teenagers out of the kingdom of darkness and into the kingdom of light.

In the same way God is amassing an international prayer army of greater size and strength than at any previous time in history. As this book is released in

November of 1997, over 50 million believers will specifically target the yet unreached peoples of our world. Surely,
God's call to His people to intercede will not be in vain.
He is not holding out the hope of revival without the
prospect of its fulfillment. Global spiritual awakening is
on the way! In fact, the first waves are already lapping the
shore.

All is **not** dark on the horizon because God is calling
His people to pray.

References

1. Ruth A. Tucker, *From Jerusalem to Irian Jaya*, Grand Rapids:
    Zondervan, 1983, p. 173.
2. Larry Stockstill, *Twenty-five Lines Around*, Baker, Louis.:
    Heartbeat Publishing, 1992, pp. 1, 2.
3. The financial power structure of the global church is rapidly
    changing; the new centers of financial strength for the
    twenty-first century church will almost certainly be in Asia,
    notably in places like South Korea, Singapore and, perhaps,
    as communism wanes, Hong Kong.

Chapter 4

Prayer
Closet World-Changers

'Ask of me,
    and I will make the nations your inheritance,
    the ends of the earth your possession.'
                                    (Psalm 2:8)

John Wesley often remarked, 'The Holy Spirit, in answer to prayer, does everything.' He also cautioned, 'You can do more than pray **after** you have prayed but you can do nothing but pray **until** you have prayed.'

This is hard for many Western Christians to learn since we tend to be activists. But since we also tend to be pragmatists, we should be praying far more than we are. Why? Because in a word, prayer works! **Prayer is the vehicle whereby the hearts of peoples and nations are prepared to receive God's offer of salvation.**

Some 50 million Christians will target the 1,739 people groups that still have no Christian witness in the massive Praying Through the Window III effort in October, 1997. Hundreds of thousands pray systematically for nations using Patrick Johnstone's *Operation World* (a goldmine of missions data) and thousands more use the excellent daily *Prayer Journal* published by Youth With A Mission. The Church Prayer Network coordinates churches to pray in cooperation with the Joshua Project 2000. The Prayer Track of the AD 2000 & Beyond movement also coordinates international prayer efforts. And the World Prayer Center and Jericho Center in Colorado Springs are gearing up for non-stop intercession until closure on the Great Commission is a reality! If Christians today are uninformed regarding prayer for nations and unreached peoples it's not because of a lack of information!

The Highest Call of All

It's especially encouraging to note that since the Praying Through the Window efforts began in the early part of this decade, the number coming to Christ every day worldwide has jumped by some 100,000 people! Dr David Barrett suggests that as many as 170 million Christians worldwide are committed to praying daily for awakening and world evangelization, and there may be as many as twenty million believers who see intercession as their primary calling.[1]

It is these unknown multitudes, not necessarily the high-profile Christians, who are well-known in the heavenlies. They are 'closet world-changers,' because from their prayer closets they are impacting the flow of history. Paul Billheimer reminds us:

'The praying people are the body politic of the world, and the church holds the balance of power in world affairs. Not only in the future ages is she the ruling and governing force in the social order, but even now, in this present throbbing moment, by means of her prayer power and to the extent to which she uses it, the praying church is actually deciding the course of human events. Some day we shall discover that prayer is the most important factor in shaping the course of human history.'[2]

Indeed, Billheimer would go on to say, 'the fate of the world is in the hands of nameless saints.'[3] Suppose that Dr Billheimer is only half right. Should that not still be sufficient motivation to move us to intercede for peoples and nations? Dick Eastman adds his voice of experience in the world prayer movement to challenge us to prayer. Eastman writes,

'I am becoming increasingly convinced that the emerging global call to pray will be the key to gathering in history's final and greatest harvest. To bring back the King, we must pray back the King.'[4]

Prayer is the vehicle whereby the hearts of peoples and nations are prepared to receive God's offer of salvation.

In fact, there is an astounding likeness between the role of prayer and closure on the Great Commission in John's apocalyptic visions in Revelation, chapters five and eight. There is a cause and effect transaction related to prayer-filled bowls and the release of angels to carry out God's directives. Seven angels are commissioned to initiate happenings that literally wrap up this present age and bring in the unmitigated rule of Jesus Christ over the earth. As a result comes the proclamation,

> *'The kingdom of the world has become the kingdom of our Lord and of His Christ, and he will reign for ever and ever.'* (Revelation 11:15)

Shortly thereafter, a loud voice from heaven declares,

> *'Now have come the salvation and the power and the kingdom of our God, and the authority of his Christ.'* (Revelation 12:10)

All of this is predicated by the prayers of saints (referred to as vials) and worship (typified by incense). In response to this glorious mix of prayer and worship, angels are set in gear to fulfill God's purposes and establish Christ's eternal rule. Beginning in chapter eight, seven angels are given trumpets that will announce God's judgment and the changing world order. But they are not permitted to use these trumpets and unfold God's purposes until something happens – until the prayers of God's people are presented before His throne. The scene is so awesome it elicits a season of silence in heaven.

> *'Another angel, who had a golden censer, came and stood at the altar. He was given much incense to offer, with the prayers of all the saints, on the golden altar before the throne. The smoke of the incense, together with the prayers of the saints, went up before God from the angel's hand.'* (Revelation 8:3, 4)

Concerning this magnificent event, Walter Wink writes,

> 'Human beings have intervened in the heavenly liturgy. The uninterrupted flow of consequences is dammed for a moment. New alternatives become

feasible. The unexpected becomes suddenly possible, because God's people on earth have invoked heaven, the home of the possible, and have been heard. What happens next, happens because people prayed. The message is clear: history belongs to the intercessors.'[5]

As a result of the prayers of God's people intermingled with their worship of the Triune God, the seven angels are released to sound their trumpets, culminating in the unrivaled inauguration of Jesus Christ as Lord over the nations and the cleansing of the nations and the colossal, final defeat of Satan, *'the accuser of our brothers'* (Revelation 12:10).

What is crucial for us to see is that apparently and astoundingly, heaven's hands are tied to complete God's end-time purposes **until** prayer and worship arise in sufficient magnitude. There is no question that one day it will happen, for Scripture says it will. The question for us is, **will we be the generation who so powerfully intercede and so potently worship that God's messengers are released to do His bidding and unfold His purposes?**

No doubt Chris Robinson and Graham Kendrick had this in mind when they wrote their great hymn, *All Heaven Waits*:

> 'All heaven waits with bated breath for saints on
>   earth to pray,
> Majestic angels ready stand with swords of fiery
>   blade.
> Astounding power awaits a word from God's
>   resplendent throne.
> But God awaits our prayer of faith that cries, "Your
>   will be done!"'[6]

The Lord's Missionary Prayers

The two prayers of our Lord recorded in John 17 and Matthew 6 are both profoundly missionary in nature.

Jesus' tender yet strong intercessory prayer for those who would believe in Him is interlaced with global evangelistic intent. In John 17:23 He specifically requests of the Father,

> *'May they be brought to complete unity to let the world know that you sent me.'*

Not coincidentally, the clarion call of the Holy Spirit to believers today is **reconciliation**. We are to be reconciled with our brothers and sisters, then we are to take up the call to be ministers of reconciliation.

> '[God] *has committed to us the message of reconciliation. We are therefore Christ's ambassadors, as though God were making His appeal through us. We implore you on Christ's behalf: Be reconciled to God.'*
>
> (2 Corinthians 5:19, 20)

Then look again at what is referred to as 'the Lord's Prayer' in Matthew 6. When taken at face value, it is clear that this too is a missionary prayer. Take another look at this oft-repeated prayer:

- *'Our Father in heaven, hallowed be your name.'* This is the **focus of missions**.
- *'Your kingdom come, your will be done on earth as it is in heaven.'* Of course, this is the **goal of missions**.
- *'Give us today our daily bread.'* This deals with the **financing of missions**.
- *'Forgive us our debts, as we also have forgiven our debtors.'* Notice that our own forgiveness is predicated

on our predetermined decision to forgive those who have wronged us. The emphasis has shifted to a great **problem of missions**: unforgiveness.

- *'And lead us not into temptation, but deliver us from the evil one.'* Here Jesus spotlights the **warfare of missions**.

- *'For Yours is the kingdom and the power and the glory forever. Amen'* (NKJV). As the prayer concludes, Jesus encourages us with the **finishing of missions**. One day the hope of His kingdom will be a reality world-wide. The earth will be filled with the glory of the Lord. But even now our hearts are filled with His glory.[7]

I encourage you to employ the Lord's missionary prayers as powerful tools of intercession for a needy world.

The Hour That Changes the World

I'm calling on you to become a 'closet world-changer.' Get alone with God and stand before Him in behalf of the nations.

But where do you begin? I've already suggested the Lord's missionary prayers as ideal launching points. But I would also suggest the following pattern as a way to powerfully influence the world right from your closet. If you pray only five minutes on each of the twelve points, you will have prayed for an hour – an hour that can change the world!

1. Pray for more workers

Jesus gives Himself a glorious title in Matthew 9:38 – Lord of the harvest. He specifically urges us to *'ask the Lord of the harvest ... to send out workers into his harvest field.'* Notice, Jesus said to pray for **workers**; not cultural analysts, not observers, not critics, but workers. Unfortunately, in some parts of the world the missionary force could be cut in half with no appreciable difference. Yet on the other hand, there is a screaming need for those who will leave their own culture to lovingly penetrate other cultures with the light and life of Jesus. These are the workers for whom Jesus said we are to pray. And, as we pray, remember that He may call you to be the answer to your own prayer!

2. Pray for those in authority
Paul wrote his son in the faith, Timothy,

> *'I urge, then, first of all, that requests, prayers, intercession and thanksgiving be made for everyone – for kings and all those in authority, that we may live peaceful and quiet lives in all godliness and holiness. This is good, and pleases God our Savior, who wants all men to be saved and to come to a knowledge of the truth.'*
>
> (1 Timothy 2:1–4)

Notice that Paul says there is a direct link between a favorable condition between the church and the state and a conducive climate for evangelism. No matter which political party is in power, Christians are biblically bound to pray for those in authority. According to Paul, God likes this! It *'pleases God our Savior.'* When governing authorities allow believers to worship and live *'peaceful and quiet lives,'* then the church can get on with its main job of evangelism.

So, let me ask you pointedly: Who's in power right now politically? Are you praying for them? It pleases God when we pray that they will come to know and follow Jesus Christ. And it pleases God when we ask that He grant wisdom to the nation's leaders so that the church will be free to pursue God's agenda. Of course, we are also free to pray that God will topple those who are obstinate to His purposes and establish righteous leadership.

3. Pray for a rapid spread of the gospel

Paul requested prayer from the Thessalonian church:

> *'Pray for us that the message of the Lord may spread rapidly and be honored.'*   (2 Thessalonians 3:1)

When we get to heaven it will be interesting to discover who paid the price in prayer for the glorious advances of the gospel in nations like South Korea. To be sure, **somebody** paid the price. Dick Eastman says,

> 'I am convinced that when we stand before God ... we will discover that every soul ever brought to a knowledge of Christ was in some way related to intercessory prayer.'[8]

Pray over your own city, asking God that the gospel prevail where you live. Pray for your pastor and ministries from your church to be anointed with evangelistic fire. Pray that you will be divinely led of God's Spirit to touch the lives of those who are hurting and in need of Jesus. Pray that the move of God's Spirit worldwide will be accelerated and that more and more people will be exposed to the gospel and say 'yes' to Christ's lordship.

4. Pray for open doors

Paul said that:

> '...a great door for effective work has opened to me, and there are many who oppose me.'
>
>   (1 Corinthians 16:9)

Faith-filled prayer can fling open doors of colossal opportunity. Pray for missionaries you know and for national workers that God will grant them exciting opportunities for the advance of the gospel.

Jesus declares,

> *'I have placed before you an open door that no one can shut.'* (Revelation 3:8)

The seemingly impregnable doors that entrap billions of Muslims, Hindus, Buddhists and animists **can** open. They **must** open. They **will** open! But they will not open **until** we 'storm the gates' in faith-filled intercession.

5. Pray for open hearts and minds
The Bible says that:

> *'...if our gospel is veiled, it is veiled to those who are perishing. The god of this age has blinded the minds of unbelievers, so that they cannot see the light of the gospel of the glory of Christ.'* (2 Corinthians 4:3, 4)

In prayer, we are to come against the spiritual darkness that has blinded unbelievers. We have been given the authority to strip the veil away so that the light of the gospel can shine.

When I began to travel a great deal by air, I became more optimistic. I soon realized that, no matter how dismal the weather may be in any given locality, when a certain altitude is reached, the sun is always shining! However, clouds lower to the surface often prevent the sun's warm light from coming through. In the same way, Satan has clouded the hearts and minds of unbelievers to the warmth of God's love for them in Christ. It is our privilege and responsibility through prayer to peel back the clouds so the Sun of righteousness can rise over the nations with healing in His wings (see Malachi 4:2).

6. Pray for boldness

When the early church got its first taste of persecution, they made a specific request to God. Feeling the heat from both the polytheistic Romans and pharisaical Jews, they prayed,

> *'Now, Lord, consider their threats and enable your servants to speak your word with great boldness.'*
>
> (Acts 4:29)

They received exactly what they requested.

> *'After they prayed, the place where they were meeting was shaken. And they were all filled with the Holy Spirit and spoke the word of God boldly.'* (Acts 4:31)

Boldness before people should be preceded with boldness before God, especially when we pray for the salvation of souls. The great prayer warrior, Ole Hallesby, wrote,

> 'Nothing makes us so bold in prayer as when we can look into the eye of God and say to Him, "Thou knowest I am not praying for personal advantage, nor to avoid hardship, nor that my own will in any way should be done, but only for this, that Thy name might be glorified."' [9]

7. Pray for divine revelation

The evangelistic strategies that will unlock peoples and nations are vouchsafed with the Holy Spirit. He will reveal those strategies to those who seek Him. In his outstanding book, *Eternity in Their Hearts*, missionary statesman Don Richardson contends that God has prepared the gospel for every culture and every culture for the gospel. With grace, cultural sensitivity and ears to hear what the Spirit is saying, we can 'crack the code' that will open peoples' hearts to the gospel.

It was divine revelation that moved the elders at Antioch to *'set apart for me Barnabas and Saul for the work to which I have called them'* (Acts 13:2). Once sent on this missionary journey, it was divine revelation that guided them in strategy for spreading the gospel. After a God-inspired vision in the night to Paul, he *'got ready at once to leave for Macedonia, concluding that God had called us to preach the gospel to them'* (Acts 16:10). The Holy Spirit desires to continue to orchestrate the gospel's advance today by granting supernatural revelation.

8. Pray for the prosperity of God's people

There is no question that some have abused what has derisively been termed 'the prosperity message.' However, it is not only legitimate but vital that we pray for the prosperity of God's people – **if** we understand prosperity's biblical purpose. David understood that Abraham's seed was under covenant edict to bring blessing to all peoples on earth (see Genesis 12:1–3). Keying off of this promise both to be blessed and to be a blessing, David prayed,

> *'May God be gracious to us and bless us*
> *and make his face shine upon us,*
> ***that your ways may be known on earth,***
> ***your salvation among all nations.'***
>> (Psalm 67:1, 2, emphasis added)

Today, as the spiritual seed of Abraham through faith in Christ, we should pray the same.

9. Pray for nations and peoples

The wonderful promise of Psalm 2:8 still holds true:

> 'Ask of me,
>   and I will make the nations your inheritance,
>   the ends of the earth your possession.'

After my father died, I walked through the stabbing grief. One day I was complaining to the Lord that, on top of losing a wonderful father, his finances (and commitments to missions) had been such that he had not left a substantial monetary inheritance. Lovingly, the Lord spoke back to my heart, 'Son, what do you **want** for an inheritance?' Immediately my heart responded, 'Lord, give me nations for my inheritance!' I believe that experience, when I was sixteen, helped launch many of the privileges of international ministry I enjoy today.

How exciting it is to know that every unreached people group on earth has now been identified and is being targeted in faith-filled prayer. In fact, most of the remaining 1,739 unreached peoples have even hosted prayer teams on-sight, in their midst (howbeit usually without their knowledge). This is our once in a lifetime opportunity. Let's turn up the intensity of our praying for a rapid spread of the gospel to all peoples!

10. Pray for the peace of Jerusalem

This is a clear biblical prayer directive from Psalm 122:6. Jerusalem has always held a major place both in history and in prophecy. Scripture says that Jesus Himself will one day touch down on the Mount of Olives and re-establish His reign from David's throne within that city. The city is a holy site for Jews, Muslims and Christians. This city was witness to Christ's sacrifice for all humanity's sins on the cross and also witness to His glorious resurrection. As we pray, we need to remember that Jerusalem is divided ethnically, politically and spiritually. In praying for the peace of this strategic city, we are praying for peace to come to all its inhabitants because of a revelation of the Prince of Peace to them.

11. Pray for Christ's exaltation

We long for Christ to be followed and adored as Lord by every tribe, language, people group and nation. One day, the joyful shout of the redeemed in heaven will be,

> *'Salvation belongs to our God, who sits on the throne, and to the Lamb ... Praise and glory and wisdom and thanks and honor and power and strength be to our God for ever and ever. Amen!'* (Revelation 7:10, 12)

But until that glorious day of culmination when Jesus shall reign, our longing prayer should be,

> *'Be exalted, O God, above the heavens,*
> *and let your glory be over all the earth.'*
>
> (Psalm 108:5)

But how will that glorious day come? Only as God pours out His Spirit on all flesh. Therefore, we must –

12. Pray for worldwide revival

Let's cry out to God,

> *'LORD, I have heard of your fame;*
> *I stand in awe of your deeds, O LORD.*
> *Renew them in our day,*
> *in our time make them known;*
> *in wrath remember mercy.'* (Habakkuk 3:2)

One day Christ will dominate the whole universe. David Bryant reminds us that 'revival is God's way of shepherding history toward great climax.'[10] An eminent theologian of colonial America, Jonathan Edwards, said,

> 'A universal dominion is pledged to Christ, and in the interim before the final consummation, the Father implements this pledge in part by successive outpourings of the Spirit...'[11]

So, come Holy Spirit! Renew Your deeds in our day, in our time make them known! Empower us for our great assignment! Oh, Lord, may Your kingdom come, may Your will be done **on earth** as it is in heaven!

And now this call to pray comes to you. Prayer is the one mission to the world that all Christians can share. As always, God is searching for 'gap people.' One of the saddest verses in the Bible is Ezekiel 22:30,

> *'I looked for a man among them who would build up the wall and stand before me in the gap on behalf of the land so I would not have to destroy it, but I found none.'*

- Will **you** stand in the gap for the nations?
- Will **you** become a 'house of prayer for all nations'?

It was a season of prayer initiated by young people – what is now referred to in history as the Haystack Prayer Meeting – that launched the world missions endeavor in America. Another prayer effort of young people throughout the Global Consultation on World Evangelization in

Seoul, Korea signaled that God is raising up a new generation of young intercessors for our day. As concerts of prayer rise to the throne from believers in every nation, we will see Satan's fortress toppled and the kingdom of God established.

Dr C. Peter Wagner often says with rejoicing that 'the international prayer movement is out of control!' Thank God, it's true! It is simply too big to quantify. And yet – and yet, there remains a desperate need for new recruits into the international prayer army. I'm calling on you today to become, in Dick Eastman's words, a 'harvest warrior' who wars for the harvest through your praying and giving.

You can be a closet world-changer. Starting today, your prayers can make a world of difference. It is the great condition of the Great Commission.

References

1. David Barrett and Todd M. Johnson, *Our Globe and How to Reach It: Seeing the World Evangelized by A.D. 2000 and Beyond*, Birmingham, Ala.: New Hope, 1990, p. 27.
2. Paul E. Billheimer, *The Technique of Spiritual Warfare*, Santa Ana, Cal.: TBN Press, 1982, p. 58.
3. Paul E. Billheimer, *Destined for the Throne*, Fort Washington, Penn.: Christian Literature Crusade, 1975, p. 106.
4. Dick Eastman, *The Jericho Hour*, Lake Mary, Fla.: Creation House, 1994, p. 25.
5. Walter Wink, 'History Belongs to the Intercessors,' *Sojourners*, October, 1990.
6. Chris Robinson and Graham Kendrick, *All Heaven Waits*, © copyright 1986, Thank You Music, PO Box 75, Eastbourne, BN23 GNW, UK.
7. The 'Lord's Prayer' as it relates to missions is discussed in further detail in Chapter 5 of my book, *A Force in the Earth*, Lake Mary, Fla.: Creation House, 1997.
8. Dick Eastman, *Love on Its Knees*, Old Tappan, New Jersey: Chosen Books, 1989, p. 19.

9. Ole Hallesby, *Prayer*, Minneapolis: Augsburg Publishing House, 1959, p. 131.
10. David Bryant, *The Hope at Hand*, Grand Rapids: Baker, 1995, p. 48.
11. *Ibid.*, p. 48.

Chapter 5

Power
And Signs Shall Follow

'But you will receive power when the Holy Spirit comes on you; and you will be my witnesses in Jerusalem, and in all Judea and Samaria, and to the ends of the earth.'   (Acts 1:8)

Some time ago an Indian pastor approached me and said, 'You don't know me, but you came and preached a gospel crusade in my city in 1988. I didn't go to your meetings,' he told me. 'In fact, I was angry that you were here. At the time I was an idol-worshiping Hindu. Whenever I would see a poster about the crusade, I wanted to tear it down. But my mother went to your meeting,' he continued. 'She had been in constant and crippling arthritic pain for many years. When you prayed in Jesus' name for the healing of the people, all the pain went out of my mother's body and never returned.'

By this time as he was relating his story, he was weeping. 'My mother returned home and told me what had happened to her. At that point, based upon her testimony, the only thing I knew about Jesus was that

He is a great healer. But her healing set me on a quest to find out more. Soon I discovered that not only is Jesus a great healer, He is a great Savior! Today I am pastoring a church back among the very Hindus I once was.'

That is the power of the gospel, the power of the living Christ. Jesus showed mercy on this man's mother, and He also saw the potential for His kingdom purposes in her son!

The vast majority of the world has a supernatural orientation. They want, need, and will accept only a gospel that comes with verifying power. According to Jesus, that is exactly the message and accompanying demonstration we are to bring. Jesus went to the synagogue and read directly out of Isaiah's prophecy,

> *'The Spirit of the Lord is on me,*
>   *because he has anointed me*
>   *to preach good news to the poor.*
> *He has sent me to proclaim freedom for the prisoners*
>   *and recovery of sight for the blind,*
> *to release the oppressed,*
>   *to proclaim the year of the Lord's favor.'*
>
> (Luke 4:18, 19)

Then He boldly proclaimed, *'Today this scripture is fulfilled in your hearing'* (Luke 4:21). Now, as Christ's ambassadors, we are to go in His name and do His works.

Early Church Missions Strategy

This is a decade rife with supernatural phenomena. In the Western world, our sterile technology has created a thirst for metaphysical experience. Many try to satiate this thirst by flirting with Eastern religions, psychic networks or the occult. Yet this thirst can never be truly satisfied until we come to the One who said, *'If anyone is thirsty, let him come to me and drink'* (John 7:37). Heaven-initiated experiences of supernatural power are the only effective Christian antidote to the proliferation of unclean, other-worldly phenomena.

As Jesus said in Acts 1:8, the fullness of the Holy Spirit is given for the purpose of effective Christian witness. The great expositor D. Martyn Lloyd-Jones saw a direct correlation between the anointing of the Holy Spirit and evangelism.

> 'Go through Acts and in every instance when we are told either that the Spirit came upon these men or that they were filled with the Spirit, you will find that it was in order to bear a witness and a testimony.'[1]

In Jesus' ministry and in the ministries of the early Christian disciples, some kind of power encounter often verified their Spirit-anointed gospel proclamation. What is a 'power encounter?' C. Peter Wagner, commenting on power encounters among tribal groups, writes that,

> 'a power encounter is a visible, practical demonstration that Jesus Christ is more powerful than the false gods or spirits worshiped or feared by a people group.'[2]

John Wimber adds,

> 'Any system or force that must be overcome for the gospel to be believed is cause for a power encounter.'[3]

At a time of acute discouragement, John the Baptist

sought reassurance that Jesus was indeed the Messiah. Jesus responded,

> *'Go back and report to John what you hear and see: The blind receive sight, the lame walk, those who have leprosy are cured, the deaf hear, the dead are raised, and the good news is preached to the poor.'* (Matthew 11:4, 5)

Jesus saw these miracles, or power encounters, as the verifying credentials of His ministry.

The New Testament model we have for the ministry of the evangelist is Philip. The report of Philip's evangelistic crusade in Samaria is also a model for biblical evangelism today.

> *'Philip went down to a city in Samaria and proclaimed the Christ there. When the crowds heard Philip and saw the miraculous signs he did, they all paid close attention to what he said. With shrieks, evil spirits came out of many, and many paralytics and cripples were healed. So there was great joy in that city.'* (Acts 8:5–8)

From this passage, we pick up key components that should be present in the ministry of a New Testament evangelist.

1. A New Testament evangelist preaches Christ

'Philip went down to a city in Samaria and proclaimed the Christ there' (Acts 8:5). Once a friend of John Wesley inquired as to the success of the meeting earlier that evening. 'What did you give them?' the friend asked. 'I gave them Christ,' Wesley responded. Ultimately, the good news concerning Jesus Christ is the only message an evangelist is allowed to deliver. I once heard a man derisively remark concerning Billy Graham, 'Well, if

you've heard him once, you've heard him!' Actually, he was paying Mr Graham a compliment. One of the beauties of hearing Billy Graham or Luis Palau is that there is no question that the gospel will be faithfully proclaimed. Sadly, such is not the case even from many evangelical and charismatic pulpits. No matter what the springboard topic may be, an evangelist's message must always end up at the same place – at the cross and the empty tomb!

2. A New Testament evangelist attracts people
The Bible says in verse six that crowds gathered to hear Philip. True evangelists possess a 'drawing' anointing.

3. A New Testament evangelist has a deliverance ministry
'With shrieks, evil spirits came out of many' (Acts 8:7). The evangelist's message of the blood of Christ is a direct assault against demonic forces. If the evangelist fully proclaims the gospel, there **ought** to be a reaction from demons! As they manifest themselves, the evangelist carries authority to drive them out in Jesus' name.

4. A New Testament evangelist has a healing ministry
'Many paralytics and cripples were healed' (Acts 8:7). A New Testament evangelist has a full appreciation of the implications of Christ's atoning work, which includes spiritual, emotional and physical healing.

> *'He himself bore our sins in his body on the tree, so that we might die to sins and live for righteousness; by his wounds you have been healed.'* (1 Peter 2:24)

5. A New Testament evangelist's ministry brings joy
'There was great joy in that city' (Acts 8:8). As people are loosed from their sins and from the power of the devil,

and as the benefits of the gospel begin to be experienced, joy can be the only result!

Notice that Philip's audience did not just hear; they **heard** and **saw**. Philip's evangelistic ministry was, first and foremost, proclaiming Christ. The preaching was augmented, however, by a deliverance ministry and the working of miracles. The Scripture suggests that the people were not convinced of the veracity of Philip's message by his preaching only. They *'paid close attention to what he said'* when they *'heard Philip and **saw** the miraculous signs he did'* (see Acts 8:6).

Paul slips his missionary strategy into his letter to the church at Rome.

> *'I will not venture to speak of anything except what Christ has accomplished through me in leading the Gentiles to obey God by what I have said and done – by the power of signs and miracles, through the power of the Spirit. So from Jerusalem all the way around to Illyricum, I have fully proclaimed the gospel of Christ. It has always been my ambition to preach the gospel where Christ was not known, so that I would not be building on someone else's foundation. Rather, as it is written: "Those who were not told about him will see, and those who have not heard will understand."'*   (Romans 15:18–21)

Paul's commitment to frontier evangelism clearly emerges in this text. He also spotlights three avenues for getting the gospel to the nations: what he says, what he does, and signs and wonders. In missionary strategy, evangelicals have emphasized what is said. The mainline denominations have stressed the social implications of the gospel (what is done). Pentecostals and charismatics have given high profile to signs and wonders. Paul said, in essence, 'I employ all three!' A careful, Spirit-orchestrated mix of word, deeds and miracles is the biblical strategy for reaching the nations.

If anyone could have relied on his academic prowess, it was Paul. Paul appeared to take the apologetics approach to evangelizing Gentiles in one place, Athens. There he won the debate with the Greek philosophers, but he lost the war; while there was limited evangelistic success, no church was planted.

I do not wish to be misunderstood. There will always be an important place for apologetics. Throughout his anointed ministry, replete with miracles, Paul continued to go to the synagogues and reason with the Jews. Nevertheless, it is probably true both then and now that for every person won to Christ through apologetics, hundreds are won through anointed proclamation and attending demonstrations of God's power.

Paul probably kicked himself spiritually all the way from Athens to Corinth. By the time he arrived, he was committed to another style of ministry than the one he used in Athens.

> 'When I came to you, brothers, I did not come with eloquence or superior wisdom as I proclaimed to you the testimony about God. For I resolved to know nothing while I was with you except Jesus Christ and him crucified. I came to you in weakness and fear, and with much trembling. My message and my preaching were not with wise and persuasive words, but with the demonstration of the Spirit's power, so that your faith might not rest on men's wisdom, but on God's power.'
>
> (1 Corinthians 2:1–5)

The writer of Hebrews also urges readers to give careful attention to their walk with the Lord.

> *'How shall we escape if we ignore such a great salvation?*
> *This salvation, which was first announced by the Lord,*
> *was confirmed to us by those who heard him. God also*
> *testified to it by signs, wonders and various miracles, and*
> *gifts of the Holy Spirit distributed according to his will.'*
>
> (Hebrews 2:3, 4)

This sampling of New Testament passages gives some indication of the place of power encounters in evangelism. A gospel that shows physical results will produce evangelistic results. T.L. Osborn probably has been used by God in power evangelism as much as any person since the first century. He says,

> 'Whether it is Peter in traditional Jerusalem, Philip in immoral Samaria, or Paul on the pagan Island of Melita, the same results always followed; they proclaimed the gospel, miracles were in evidence, and multitudes believed and were added to the church.'[4]

Throughout the world the Holy Spirit is employing the same strategy today.

The Rationale for Miracles

Signs and wonders are not meant to be ends in themselves. The purpose of a sign is to point people in a definite direction. The purpose of a supernatural sign is to point people to Jesus Christ. A wonder is intended to bring the element of wonder into Christianity. Wonders help guard the Christian faith from degenerating into stale, rationalistic propositions.

The release of signs and wonders help people turn from falsehood to the true and living God. This happens in several important ways. First, **miracles reveal God's glory**. God demonstrated His power to Pharaoh and his diviners in order to destroy the people's confidence in the false gods of Egypt. God stretched out His hand in power across Egypt *'so you may know that the earth is the LORD's'* (Exodus 9:29).

Second, **miracles reveal Jesus Christ as God in human flesh**. John 20:30, 31 says,

> *'Jesus did many other miraculous signs in the presence of his disciples, which are not recorded in this book. But these are written that you may believe that Jesus is the Christ, the Son of God, and that by believing you may have life in his name.'*

Third, **miracles reveal God's mercy**. Whenever Jesus stretched out His hand in healing, He was displaying God's compassionate heart. As the people saw God's character and disposition of love, they wanted to respond in love and faith to Him. No wonder Paul was an exponent of power evangelism.

> *'Our gospel came to you not simply with words, but also with power, with the Holy Spirit and with deep conviction.'*   (1 Thessalonians 1:5)

The Great Commission's Punch

For many, the gospel of redemption does not begin with New Testament stories but with humanity's loss of authority in the beginning. I once discussed this with T.L. Osborn. He explained to me that his method of evangelistic preaching in over seventy nations has been to apply to contemporary life a miracle story from the ministry of Jesus. In each message he explains:

1. God's good creation;
2. What Satan has done to destroy and pervert God's good creation; and
3. How Jesus has redeemed what the devil sought to destroy.

In other words, our point of entry in gospel preaching goes back further than much historic evangelistic preaching. The message does not start with redemption; rather, it culminates with redemption. Ours is a message of restoration. Since the cross God has been 'crescendoing' His redemptive and restorative work.

> *'The reason the Son of God appeared was to destroy the devil's work.'* (1 John 3:8)

And this good news comes with attesting power. As Peter Wagner states,

> 'Across the board, the most effective evangelism in today's world is accompanied by manifestations of supernatural power.'[5]

Another look at the Great Commission reveals that every statement of it is accompanied by a promise of power. In Matthew 28:18, 19, before Jesus says *'Go and make disciples of all nations,'* He says, *'All authority in heaven and on earth has been given to me.'* In Mark 16:15, 17, Jesus commands His disciples to preach the gospel to every person. Then He promises, *'And these signs will accompany those who believe.'* In Luke 24, He tells His disciples that they will be witnesses of the things they have seen. But first they must *'stay in the city until you have been clothed with power from on high'* (v. 49). In John 20:21, 22, Jesus says to His disciples, *'As the Father has sent me, I am sending you.'* Then immediately He breathed on them and said, *'Receive the Holy Spirit.'* Acts 1:8 is a rebuke to activism without accompanying spiritual power. How motivated the disciples must have been when the resurrected Christ commanded them to evangelize the world! But then He cooled His disciples' heels, in essence saying, *'Go ... but not yet.'* Before they become His witnesses, they were to receive power when the Holy Spirit would come on them. That same power is available to us today.

1. We have the **power of the gospel**. Paul said,

> *'I am not ashamed of the gospel, because it is the power of God for the salvation of everyone who believes.'*
>
> (Romans 1:16)

2. We have the **power of the Word of God**. Not only is the Bible cross-cultural; it transcends cultures. The Bible is not judged by the yardstick of any culture. Rather, all cultures are judged by the standard of the Bible.

> *' "Is not my word like fire," declares the LORD, "and like a hammer that breaks a rock in pieces?" '*
>
> (Jeremiah 23:29)

3. We have the **power of the name of Jesus**. Every knee will one day bow before His name. When interrogated for the healing of the lame man, Peter replied,

> *'By faith in the name of Jesus, this man whom you see and know was made strong. It is Jesus' name and the faith that comes through him that has given this complete healing to him, as you can all see.'*
>
> (Acts 3:16)

4. We have the **power of the blood of Jesus**. Christians have every right to 'plead the blood' against any design of the enemy.

    'They overcame him by the blood of the Lamb and by the word of their testimony; they did not love their lives so much as to shrink from death.' (Revelation 12:11)

5. We have the **power of the Holy Spirit**. Evangelism is a sovereign work. The Holy Spirit is the great evangelist. The best laid plans of men and women are inadequate if the breath of God's life doesn't animate them. Evangelistic effectiveness is *'"Not by might nor by power, but by my Spirit," says the LORD Almighty'* (Zechariah 4:6).

    The power of the Holy Spirit is the definitive edge in effective evangelism. Charles Kraft, professor of anthropology and intercultural communication at Fuller Seminary, addresses this:

    'Jesus' kingdom people are to receive the Spirit of the Lord as He did, through the infilling of the Holy Spirit (Luke 3:21–22). Then in the power and authority given by God, we are like Jesus, to release poor, captive, blind and oppressed people from the enemy because God values and loves His creatures. For "the time has come" when God will rescue those who have fallen under the evil influence of Satan. Jesus assumes conflict and enlists us in His war. Then we, like Jesus, are to use God's power to demonstrate God's love.'[6]

With Signs Following

God is clearly at work in dramatic ways around the world. I recently returned from the Pacific island nation of Fiji, where the church is in the throes of revival. God is using Bible college students as well as seasoned ministers to display His power. One Fijian student named Nina had gone to Papau New Guinea to do village evangelism. She discovered a village almost totally under the control of demons. She simply began to lay hands on the people, including the children, commanding evil spirits to leave in Jesus' name. Immediately people began to be healed of long-standing infirmities and some who were deaf began to hear. An old man who just sat observing all of this determined that he would speak out against this move of God's Spirit. But as he began to speak, he fell from his chair and was unable to open his mouth. He repented and opened his heart to Christ. Another woman, who had drunk a concoction of betel juice prepared by a witch doctor, had a choking lump in her throat ever since she drank the potion. But when she renounced all witchcraft and opened her heart to Christ, the lump immediately disappeared. These notable healings softened the hearts of the entire village toward the Lord and many were swept into the kingdom of God.[7]

Now, entire books are being written about signs and wonders including Jane Rumph's excellent book, *Stories From the Front Lines: Power Evangelism in Today's World* (Chosen Books, 1996). Included are multiple accounts of divine healing, prophecy, dreams and visions, miracles and encounters with angels.

Let us never forget that all of these wonders from God's hand are for a specific purpose – the advance of the gospel and making disciples of all nations. At Pentecost, Peter pointed the curious to Calvary. Demonstrations of power that become ends in themselves disconnect from the spirit of the gospel. If we emphasize Pentecostal potency without Calvary's cross eventually we get power without love. And power without love always turns brutal. **Jesus**, not healing, is our message. **Jesus**, not miracles, is our message. Dare I say it? **Jesus**, not prosperity, is our message! Yes, without question, Jesus brings all of the above. But the message, the focus, the attraction is **Him**!

Now, as in the church's inception, the great missions need is not greater harvest but more laborers. I do not believe that God's desire is merely to empower select individuals to experience the miraculous. He longs to empower His whole church! *'You shall receive power when the Holy Spirit comes on you.'* **The power of the Holy Spirit verifies the gospel and enables us to be Christ's witnesses to the ends of the earth**. Notice that it wasn't gifted healing evangelists that were the first wave of missionary advance; it was the everyday followers of Jesus, just like you and me.

'Then the disciples went out and preached everywhere, and the Lord worked with them and confirmed his word by the signs that accompanied it.' (Mark 16:20)

References

1. D. Martyn Lloyd-Jones, *Joy Unspeakable*, Eastbourne, England: Kingsway, 1984, p. 75.
2. C. Peter Wagner, 'Special Kinds of Church Growth', Class notes, Fuller Theological Seminary, 1984, p. 14.
3. John Wimber with Kevin Springer, *Power Evangelism*, San Francisco: Harper and Row, 1986, p. 16.
4. T.L. Osborn, *The Harvest Call*, Tulsa, Okla.: The Voice of Faith, 1953, p. 143.
5. C. Peter Wagner, *The Third Wave of the Holy Spirit*, Ann Arbor, Mich.: Vine Books, 1988, p. 87.
6. Charles E. Kraft, *Christianity With Power*, Ann Arbor, Mich.: Vine Books, 1988, p. 110.
7. From a personal conversation with Robert Abramson, missionary to Fiji, in June, 1997.

Chapter 6

Partnership
Healing Our Self-Inflicted Wounds

'That all of them may be one, Father, just as you are in me and I am in you. May they also be one in us so that the world may believe that you have sent me.' (John 17:21)

It was a turning point in our hopes for world evangelization when Dr Avery Willis, representing the International Mission Board of the Southern Baptist Convention, humbled himself in behalf of his denomination before the 4000 delegates to the Global Consultation on World Evangelization in Seoul, Korea. I sat in that crowd of world mission leaders as I heard Dr Willis apologize on behalf of Southern Baptists for provincialism and a lack of cooperation and partnership in missions.

Dr Willis's generous act is indicative of a new spirit that is alive and well within the missions community. As a new spirit of partnership emerges among agencies, denominations and mission-hearted Christians around the world, we should be filled with gratitude. God is weaving together a force in the earth to take full advantage of this once in a lifetime mega-harvest.

The famous missionary, Amy Carmichael, left her homeland for India. She rescued many children from the prostitution rings that were rampant in Hindu temples at the time. Almost immediately, Amy began to fit into the Indian culture. She never heard the term 'culture shock' and it is unlikely that she experienced it. There was another shock, however, that was almost fatal for young Amy. Upon arriving in the mission field in India, Amy was shocked to discover that missionaries did not love one another. She learned, as well, that efforts are often stymied by our refusal to forgive. Unforgiveness brings serious consequences.

> *'For if you forgive men when they sin against you, your heavenly Father will also forgive you. But if you do not forgive men their sins, your Father will not forgive your sins.'* (Matthew 6:14, 15)

Our only hope of seizing this *kairos* moment in missions is to partner with all world Christians and link arms to gather the glorious harvest.

What the Spirit is Saying to the Churches

If there is one irrefutable message God is speaking to the body of Christ today it is **reconciliation**. We are to be reconciled across denominational, racial, gender and national barriers, demonstrating the true spiritual unity for which Jesus so passionately prayed in John 17.

Having been reconciled with our brothers and sisters, we are then to take up the call to be ministers of reconciliation. **Reconciliation is at the heart of the missions mandate**.

As God has grown the church to be a truly global community, all vestiges of racism must now cease. Incisive Christians believe that the root sin of the United States is racism. Billy Graham agrees. In a recent interview, when he was asked what one sin he wished he could eradicate from the world, he answered racial strife.

Jesus forcefully attacked the ethnic pride and provincialism of His own disciples by forcing them to travel through Samaria and interact with the Samaritans. Jesus' ministry to the woman at the well is a clear indication of how He Himself lovingly reached across ethnic and gender barriers to meet the needs of this precious, victimized woman. Later in ministry to the Samaritan village Jesus showed tremendous compassion and quickly accepted the Samaritan's invitation to stay in their village for a few days (much to the disciples' chagrin, no doubt).

Jesus was kicking the provincialism out of His disciples then and He continues to kick the provincialism out of His disciples today. If you are going to be a disciple of Jesus and follow Him, you follow where He leads, and where He is leading is into uncomfortable territory to interact with those whom you may not even like and with whom you share no common heritage.

As ambassadors of Jesus Christ we are called upon to be ministers of reconciliation. Certainly, at its very core, we are to be proclaimers of the gospel that reconciles people to God. But we also are to exhibit a lifestyle of reconciliation. John Dawson, in his outstanding book, *Healing America's Wounds*, gives specific steps to being a true minister of reconciliation:

1. **Take the opportunity of confession, with identification, when you find it**. We will have begun the healing when we realize that we are at least partly responsible for any unfinished business with God or offended persons. He reminds us,

'Sometimes a few humble words can begin a dramatic word of healing.'

2. **Release forgiveness and refrain from judgment**. We must bring our own wounded spirit to Jesus if we are to be used by Him as reconcilers. John Dawson asserts,

> 'Racism and all the other prejudicial attitudes could be eradicated from the intercessor's heart if we simply give the other person, group or race the benefit of the doubt. Leave the judgment to God; refrain from coming to conclusions about the motives behind actions.'

3. **Receive God's gifts of friendship**. God organizes and builds His Kingdom through gifts of friendship.
4. **Join united efforts**. When the different streams of God's Spirit converge, they flow together as an irresistible tide.
5. **Look for opportunities to move past your own local church and even your own denomination**.
6. **Look around**. Seek to understand the times and seasons as Daniel did. John Dawson says,

> 'It will take an informed mind and an enlarged heart to embrace the ambition of God for the people of America.'

The same could be said for the people of any nation. He continues,

> 'In addition to the foundational truths held by all the orthodox streams, there are the unique flashes of light shed by each. There is more than a division of labor in the Body of Christ. A division

of emphasis also makes possible a wide view of a wide subject: God.'

7. **Hold your ground**. If you are to believe God, that which we have not yet seen manifested will stretch our faith to birth a multi-generational blessing at the womb of today's circumstances.[1]

God is calling you to be a minister of reconciliation. You are to start in the not-so-little ways that the Holy Spirit would speak to your heart even now. Are there any festering wounds you have toward other believers that are not yet healed? Get it right today, then become an agent of reconciliation to others.

Friends Become Partners

As the church's center of gravity continues to shift from Western nations to Latin America, Asia and Africa, there is much give and take and many fabulous lessons we are learning from one another. I've had the privilege of worshiping with the body of Christ on every continent. Hues of color, diversity and emphasis only underscore to me the beauty of Christ's bride, His church. We must proactively become friends with one another, honoring the strengths that come from the church in every nation. Fellowship is based upon our theological foundation of having the same Father. We have been born of the same Spirit and purchased by the same precious blood of our Lord Jesus. The Western church learns humility and faith from the church of the Two-Thirds World. The church of the Two-Thirds World learns vision and structure from the Western church. Who benefits? The kingdom of God benefits!

Maurice Sinclair challenges us to a courageous partnership for the world harvest.

'How can we partner in mission in a way which squares with that of the patriarchs, prophets, apostles, and, above all, with that of Jesus Christ? How can we take our place alongside those who have gone before us and be worthy heirs of the missionary inheritance? How, if at all, can we relate to the different continents and different kinds of localities today, and give and receive help from fellow Christians in these other places? How, locally and across the globe, can we weave a Christian network which shows beauty, just and loving relationships worth copying because they are better than the interconnections of the secular world? Four questions as big as these yield to a one word answer: Partnership!' [2]

Friendship in missions has a long and glorious history, punctuated with various ethics of selfish ambition. However, even back in the days of the apostle Paul, Paul commends the Philippian church as being *'loyal yoke-fellows'* who have *'labored side by side'* with him in the gospel. The Philippians had entered into partnership with Paul on his missionary endeavors by sending him material support. By doing so, they have also entered into his suffering as Paul himself has experienced the fellowship of the suffering of Christ.

With a few notable exceptions in the Western world, Christians today are experiencing one of three phases of attack: harassment, persecution, or martyrdom. It is clear that we are to rejoice with those who rejoice and weep with those who weep. As we identify with the body of Christ, holding hands as friends and then as partners in advancing the gospel to the 1,739 yet unreached peoples of our world, we see God's hand of grace and share both the sufferings and the triumphs of the church around the world.

Farewell to Western Dominated Missions

The first Lausanne International Congress on World Evangelization hardly mentioned Pentecostals and charismatics. Further, it was primarily a gathering of a predominantly white 'good old boy' network of leaders of Western missionary agencies. I do not mean to be disparaging, as this was an important and noble first attempt. Nor am I suggesting that the 1974 Lausanne Congress was limited because of its composition of delegates. In fact, it became a springboard for much of the advance of the gospel into the Two-Thirds world. Further, the historic document that was drafted from this conference, The Lausanne Covenant, has been something of a theological battle cry for world evangelization ever since.

Section 8 of the Covenant, titled *Churches in Evangelistic Partnership*, still carries tremendous importance for us today.

'God is raising up from the younger churches a great new resource for world evangelization, and is thus demonstrating that the responsibility to evangelize belongs to the whole Body of Christ. All churches should therefore be asking God and themselves what they should be doing both to reach their own area and to send missionaries to other parts of the world. A re-evaluation of our missionary responsibility and roll should be continuous. Thus, a growing partnership of churches will develop and the universal character of Christ's church will be more clearly exhibited. We also thank God for agencies which labor in Bible translation, theological education, the mass media, Christian literature, evangelism, missions, church renewal, and other specialist fields.

They too should engage in constant self-examination to evaluate their effectiveness as part of the Church's mission.'

God is raising up three-fold chords of partnership for world harvest. Maurice Sinclair reminds us,

'For the global partnership to work, it must be a partnership of reconciliation, understanding, actuality, prayer and suffering. Only then will it fully and truly be a partnership of reaping.'[3]

The role of the Western church in missions is changing dramatically. That is why God called me at the beginning of the 1990s to stop conducting my own evangelistic crusades to other nations. Rather, He instructed me to 'lift up the hands' of national pastors, evangelists and church leaders in order to enable them to fulfill their God-given dreams and visions for the harvest. Since that time, Global Advance has provided training and tools for over 100,000 native pastors and church leaders in over 30 nations. God has given us a vision to train one million leaders to plant one million new churches worldwide. Our new role is to affirm, undergird, encourage and partner with indigenous churches and their leadership around the world.

The first Lausanne Congress on World Evangelization in 1974 was dominated by missions executives from Western nations, primarily the United States. By 1989, when the second Lausanne Congress was held in Manila, major changes were afoot in the global church. Delegates now came from over 150 nations and nearly 50 percent of the participants had some kind of Pentecostal or charismatic orientation.

But the biggest surprise was still ahead. The first and

second Lausanne Congresses provided 'snapshots' of the complexion of the broad evangelical movement world-wide. The third 'snapshot' of the composition of global evangelicalism was the Global Consultation on World Evangelization in Seoul, Korea, in 1995. This gathering revealed two dramatic changes. First, the majority of the world's evangelicals are no longer from Western nations but rather from developing nations. Second, the majority of the world's evangelicals now are some stripe of Pente-costal or charismatic. In other words, God has added two new elements to today's typical evangelical: color and charismata! Changes in the makeup of global evangel-icalism have been astounding. The message from God's Spirit to all of us is clear. We need one another. The Western church needs the Two-Thirds World church. The Two-Thirds World church needs the Western church. They need our fellowship, not just our money. We need their wisdom, not just their anointing.

'We are all members of one body.'   (Ephesians 4:25)

It has been suggested by some that the new role of American Christians in missions is simply to sponsor mission projects overseas and help fund the younger, more vibrant churches of the Two-Thirds World. While I agree that partnership certainly includes a financial element, I believe it mocks true partnership simply to throw money at Two-Thirds World churches. My first line of identity is not as an American but as a world Christian. Nevertheless, I cannot hide who I am, nor do I seek to. I am an Anglo-American. I am a beneficiary of the legacy of my ethnicity, including both its sins and triumphs. I am fully aware that indigenous churches and indigenous leaders are at the heart of God's plan for the evangel-ization of the yet unreached peoples. However, I also understand that the final missions thrust mandates a penetration from outside the culture with the gospel. You will have to take the Great Commission out of my Bible for me not to believe that I too am mandated to go! Western Christians as well are under high orders from the King of kings to go into all the world, preach the gospel and make disciples of all the nations.

There is still a place for Western missionaries. However, there is no place for any Western missionary who wears the grave clothes of colonialism, provincialism or paternalism. The new role of Western missionaries is as the junior partner, strengthening the hands and affirming the vision of the Two-Thirds World church.

Mission's Three-Fold Chords

The Bible says,

> *'A cord of three strands is not quickly broken.'*
> (Ecclesiastes 4:12)

God is orchestrating several 'three-fold chords' in missions today.

The three-fold cord of ministry
In Romans 15:18, 19, Paul said,

> '[he led] *the Gentiles to obey God by what I have said and done – by the power of signs and miracles, through the power of the Holy Spirit.'*

Here Paul spotlights three avenues for getting the gospel to the nations: word, deeds, and signs and wonders. In missionary strategy, traditional evangelicals have emphasized proclamation (word). The mainline denominations have stressed the social implications of the gospel (deeds). Pentecostals and charismatics have given high profile to signs and wonders. Paul said, in essence, 'I employ all three!' A careful, Spirit-orchestrated mix of word, deeds and miracles is the biblical strategy for reaching the nations.

The three-fold cord of prayer

Three strands are also being woven together by the believer's ministry in the heavenlies. The ministry of **intercession** before God for the nations is being intertwined in ministry to the Lord in **praise and worship**. An aggressive, **spiritual warfare** against principalities and powers contends for long-held territories and entire nations. The ministry of intercession with its focus on the lost, praise and worship with its focus on the Lord, and spiritual warfare with its focus on engaging principalities and powers is a powerful three-fold cord for the harvest.

The three-fold cord of churches

A three-fold cord of distinctive churches is now being intertwined by the Holy Spirit for the global harvest. First there are the historic denominational churches. Then there are also the newer evangelical churches, both Pentecostal and non-Pentecostal that would be part of the evangelical makeup of churches in most nations. In my own nation, this second strand would represent churches affiliated with the National Association of Evangelicals. But the third and newest strand may be the most exciting of all – the 'new apostolic' churches. While these churches are predominantly charismatic, the new apostolic churches would also cover such powerful moves of God's Spirit as the Willow Creek Community Church phenomenon. Sometimes referred to as 'post-denominational' churches, these younger churches throughout the world represent by far the fastest-growing segment of Christianity. However, the new apostolic churches are learning to acknowledge their tremendous debt to the older evangelical and mainline denominational churches. Together they form a powerful three-fold cord.

It has been estimated that there are some nine million Christian churches worldwide. It has also been suggested by several missions analysts that at least another nine million churches are needed to bring closure on the Great Commission. If this three-fold cord of churches continues to entwine, together we can see 'a church for every people' within the next few years.

Three-fold cord of generations

God is weaving a strong cord of at least three generations of missions leadership: older, younger, and the young. The great, post-war leadership of the church is fast departing from the scene. The death last year of Lester Sumrall and other charismatic pioneers signals a passing of the torch to men and women in my age bracket who represent the younger leadership. We are not the post World War II era of leadership. Many of us are products of the Jesus Movement of the late sixties and early seventies. God is raising up a powerful cadre in my own nation of mission leaders among this younger group, such as Ted Haggard, George Otis, Jr, Cindy Jacobs, Larry Stockstill and John Dawson. However, we too are in our mid-40s and beyond. Now the Holy Spirit has His eye on the young. I believe those sometimes referred to as Generation *X* are poised to make the greatest contribution to missions of any generation in Christian history. God has raised up ministries like Teen Mania to help produce a generation of missions leadership for a life-sized challenge. Ron Luce, founder of Teen Mania, understands God's call to youth.

'This generation is waiting for the challenge that will demand their all. They have become disillusioned with both the secular world and the Christian world. In its natural resources – the vision and the energy of a whole generation of youth – are being squandered. We must show them a Christianity that will answer their cry for a meaningful life.

It is time to call them to give their lives away for a cause greater than themselves. We need to let them know there is a Christ to live for a cause worth dying for.' [4]

God has specifically spoken to me to invest my life in this young generation of emerging missions leadership. That is why I've committed the first half of 1999 to a world tour of Bible colleges. I want to pour my heart and passion into emerging church leaders around the world. And I want to hear their hearts as well. I want to lay hands on them and them to lay hands on me. The Holy Spirit wants to link generations of missions leadership for the greatest global harvest ever.

Three-fold cord of agencies

Because of the demise of communism in the former Soviet Union, a political vacuum emerged in the early 1990s and continues to influence politics around the world. What is important for us, however, is to see that there is an enduring and endearing relationship as the Holy Spirit links a three-fold chord of missions cultures: European missions, US-dominated missions, and global church missions.

The great new missions fact of our time is the internationalization of the church and ownership of the Great Commission by churches around the world. In fact, there are now more missionaries being deployed from the

Two-Thirds World than from Western nations.[5] Missionaries from these developing nations are sometimes poor, spiritually radical and often juxtaposed to the wealthy, middle-aged conservative church of the West. The new missions force is much more in touch with poverty, oppression and the supernatural. The new base of Christianity is in the southern hemisphere and this is producing new missions methodology. Alex Aerugo, an executive with Partners International, comments,

> 'US evangelicals will continue to have a significant presence in the 21st Century, but it will be quite a different missions century. They will continue to bring a significant portion of the resources and support services personnel, but they will not be able to maintain alone their leadership in decision making, expertise, and field personnel. The church in the non-western world has come into world missions to stay.'[6]

The quickest way to reach the unreached peoples of our world is through partnership as churches in the West partner with churches and new missions agencies in developing nations. Dr Howard Foltz, president of the Association of International Missions Services (AIMS) writes,

> 'The churches in the West will be wise to learn how to partner with churches in developing nations for cooperative ventures to reach "third party" groups of unreached peoples. If we do not learn how to do this we will be left behind, because God is dancing on the grave, so to speak, of the colonial approach to missions work. He is going on with partnership strategies and cross-cultural teamwork.'[7]

Partnering together for the harvest can become our strongest asset for reaping the greatest possible harvest. Grant McClung challenges us all:

> 'Let's globalize the doctrinal process and ask Asian Indian Pentecostals to help us with the New Age Movement (reworked Hinduism, customized for a European and American audience). Let's get Asian, African and Latin American pastors and evangelists on our Bible conference and retreat programs to talk to us about spiritual warfare, signs and wonders, and "power evangelism." Let's continue to encourage faculty exchanges with the "third church" to learn about theology through Third World eyes. Let's call for the aggressive missionary evangelists from the burgeoning Third World Pentecostal churches to "come over to Macedonia and help us." '[8]

There is a tragic story of a little boy who had gone outside to play in the snow. Suddenly the snowfall reached blizzard dimensions and the little boy was lost in a gigantic snow drift. Alarmed, both parents ran outside through the large field next to their home, searching for their son. They even telephoned neighbors to come and assist in looking for the lost child. Independently and intensely many continued to look for the little boy, but to no avail. Finally it was determined that all of the volunteers in the field should take hands and walk across the field together. Only then could they rescue the lost boy. Resolutely, they determined to lock arms and walk the field together. They did find the lost little boy – but it was too late. He had frozen to death as many people were frantically, yet independently, looking for him.

May God help us to lock arms together and partner to rescue this generation, before it's too late.

References

1. John Dawson, *Healing America's Wounds*, Ventura, Calif.: Regal Books, 1994, pp. 19–28.
2. Maurice Sinclair, *Ripening Harvest, Gathering Storm*, London: MARC/STL Books, 1988, p. 201.
3. Maurice Sinclair, *Ibid.*, p. 209.
4. Ron Luce, *Inspire the Fire*, Lake Mary, Fla.: Creation House, 1994, p. 60.
5. Andres Tapia, 'New Look for Missionaries,' *Christianity Today*, October 4, 1993, p. 64.
6. Alex Aerugo, 'Retooling for the Future,' *Evangelical Missions Quarterly*, October, 1993, p. 362.
7. Howard Foltz, *Triumph: Mission Renewal for the Local Church*, Joplin, Mo.: Messenger Books, 1994, p. 167.
8. Grant McClung, 'The Pentecostal "Trunk" Must Learn from Its "Branches",' *Evangelical Missions Quarterly*, January, 1993, p. 38.

Chapter 7

Potential
Throwing Your Life Into the Harvest

> *'Now to him who is able to do immeasurably more than all we ask or imagine, according to his power that is at work within us, to him be glory in the church and in Christ Jesus throughout all generations, for ever and ever! Amen.'*
> (Ephesians 3:20–21)

A scene from my first trip to India seared my heart. One day I watched from a distance as a young girl, perhaps ten years old, dodged her way across a crowded street. She was obviously malnourished; her protruding stomach contrasted sharply with the rest of her emaciated frame. She carried a large tray piled high with fruit and vegetables. She darted past tons of protected protein – India's sacred cows. Finally, on the side of the road, she knelt and offered the tray of food at a small shrine – to rot in front of her 'hungry' deities. That day I saw clearly that this social evil was not the result of bad economics but bad theology.

For this reason I have little sympathy for some of the ill-informed bleeding hearts of the Western world who view Christian persuaders as villains for challenging the long-established religions of other lands. I make no apologies for being a Christian persuader. Christianity, by its very nature, is evangelistic. We are on a rescue mission with eternal consequences.

The great theologian Emil Brunner said, 'The church exists by mission as fire exists by burning.' Yet, sadly, many in the church today do not seem to have a clue as to God's purposes, either for them or for their world.

Contrast this with a conversation I had with a young man who had recently come to Christ out of the surfing scene in southern California. He told me, 'David, I didn't grow up in church. My family never went to church even on Easter or Christmas. I never attended a Sunday school class. I never heard a sermon except for a few sentences as I was surfing the channels on television. I have had no Christian orientation. But since I have received Christ I've been reading the Bible ferociously. I'm still growing and there are a lot of things I still don't understand. But it didn't take me long to realize that Jesus left His church a job to do.'

Here is a young man with no Christian upbringing whatsoever. Yet with his first orientation to Christianity he understands that Jesus has given a specific assignment to those who follow Him. How is it that many of us who have been in the church for decades still haven't figured that out? God put you here on purpose – His purpose. He saved you on purpose – His purpose. He did not merely give you a fire insurance policy to keep you out of hell when you came to faith in Christ. There is a specific something God wants your life to accomplish and only you can do it.

Missions' Motives

'But wait a minute,' you may be saying. 'Doesn't something have to happen on the inside of you for you to be excited and involved in world missions?' You're absolutely right! And in the next few minutes, if you will allow the Holy Spirit permission, He will do a major work in your heart so that your heart aligns with His.

I recently saw an amazing illustration of this on educational television. Two human hearts had literally been extracted from the chest cavities of their donors. Both hearts were beating independently. However, when one heart was tied to the other, the rhythms came to be in perfect sync. This is the way it is when we tie our heart to the heart of God. We stop marching to our own drum beat. We stop listening to our own life rhythms. Instead, we step in cadence with the heartbeat and the rhythm of God.

In all our activity the bottom line is that we do what we are stirred to do. Are there some drives, born in the heart of God, that can propel you into greater missions involvement? Indeed there are.

1. We should be involved in missions out of a *sense of obligation*

Paul felt acutely indebted to his generation. He exposes one of the great driving forces of his life when he says, *'I am obligated'* (Romans 1:14). Those enlightened by the gospel have a profound responsibility to those still in darkness. When we understand our debt we too will say, *'I am eager to preach the gospel ... I am not ashamed of the gospel'* (Romans 1:15–16).

I received Jesus Christ into my life as a little boy in vacation Bible school on 12 June, 1953. I still remember scenes from that day. I remember what appeared to be hundreds of children, singing songs to Jesus, including this one:

> Into my heart, into my heart,
> Come into my heart, Lord Jesus.
> Come in today. Come in to stay.
> Come into my heart, Lord Jesus.

I also remember Mrs Gertrude Nathan telling us the wonderful story of God's love and salvation in Jesus Christ. Then I remember kneeling at an old-time altar at the front, and praying that eternity-altering prayer:

> 'Lord Jesus, thank You for dying on the cross for me. Right now, I turn away from all my sins. Come into my heart, Lord Jesus. Take my sins away. I want to be Your child from now on. Help me to live for You all the days of my life.'

A few years ago I was back at that very church where decades earlier I had first opened my heart to Christ. I walked into the auditorium in the afternoon when no one was there. It looks much the same as it did in 1953. I walked to the front and knelt at the altar, at the very place where my life had been so wonderfully changed. I just knelt and worshiped, thanking God again for so great salvation. And then I made a fresh commitment that I would spend the rest of my life getting what happened to me there . . . to others.

If it is not a physical place, I pray that there is a place in your heart that you go back to and you let this sense of obligation work in you again. Since we have received the blessings of the gospel we are clearly obligated to get those blessings to others.

2. We should be involved in missions out of a *sense of devotion*

'For Christ's love compels us' (2 Corinthians 5:14). Christ's love for us and our love for Him always thrusts us into the harvest. There is no such thing as Christian discipleship that is not evangelistic. According to Jesus Himself the result of following Him is that we become 'fishers of men' and women (Matthew 4:19).

Two hundred and fifty years ago, there was a wealthy, titled man by the name of Nikolas Von Zinzendorf. Zinzendorf gave refuge to a group of very committed Christians called the Moravians. The Moravians were so committed to the evangelization of the world that several of them voluntarily sold themselves into slavery. When asked why, they said, 'Simply for the high privilege of preaching Christ to these precious people.' At any given time, at least fifty percent of the Moravians were serving Jesus Christ in cross-cultural missions. They began a prayer meeting for the evangelization of the world that went seven days a week, twenty-four hours a day, nonstop for 100 years. Such was the devotion of the Moravians. What compelled them to do it? What drove them to this level of devotion? Over and over, Zinzendorf challenged them to 'go and win for the Lamb the reward of His sacrifice.' He was pointing the Moravians beyond the task to the honor of Jesus Himself.

We are currently in a once in a lifetime opportunity regarding world evangelization. Nevertheless, I would not want you to think that I am merely championing a cause, even a cause as noble as the evangelization of the world. What I am urging upon all of us is that we so freshly fall in love with Jesus Christ that what is precious to Him becomes precious to us and what is priority for Him becomes priority for us. Jesus is very clear about what that is. He said,

> *'The Son of Man has come to seek and to save that which was lost.'* (Luke 19:10 NKJV)

3. We should be involved in missions out of a *sense of destiny*

World evangelization becomes an integrating theme around which all other concerns orbit. When interrogated by King Agrippa, Paul was able to reply,

> *'I was not disobedient to the vision from heaven. First to those in Damascus, then to those in Jerusalem and in all Judea, and to the Gentiles also, I preached that they should repent and turn to God and prove their repentance by their deeds.'* (Acts 26:19–20)

We are a chosen generation. That for which 2000 years Christians have prayed and hoped lies within our reach – closure on Christ's Great Commission. God has allowed your life to intersect with one of the most exciting times in all history. We have the privilege of helping set the time table of heaven's eschatology. In times like these, God's word calls us to both holiness and evangelism. **It is time for every Christian and every church to be awakened to their full and thrilling potential**.

> *'But you are a chosen people, a royal priesthood, a holy nation, a people belonging to God, that you may declare the praises of him who called you out of darkness into his wonderful light.'* (1 Peter 2:9)

Christians have been reading that verse for almost 2000 years but if ever there should be a generation that would read it and say, 'He is talking about **us**,' it should be this generation. We are indeed people of destiny and God has brought you to the kingdom for such a time as this.

The new missions leadership that drafted the GCOWE '95 Declaration understands this. Hear well these stirring words from the Declaration:

'We confess a deep awareness of our failure in the past to do all we could have done to make Christ known throughout the world, especially in the areas where no church movement exists. We also repent of our needless divisions and competitive attitudes that have hindered the advance of the Gospel. We resolve, by God's grace, to no longer ignore the challenges, nor miss the opportunities set before us. This is the time for which we were born (Esther 4:14).'

Finding Where You Fit

I am often rebuffed when I challenge Christians in this way with the statement, 'Well, not every Christian is called to be a missionary.' I tend to agree. Not everyone of us has giftings in cross-cultural ministry. However, **every Christian** is called to be a witness for Jesus Christ and **every Christian** is called to missions. There is a difference between being called to be a **missionary** and being called to **missions**. Not every believer has the missionary gift, but every Christian is called to some kind of involvement in missions. We are all called to advance the gospel in some way and to participate in the fulfilling of God's purposes in our generation.

There is a role God wants you to play in helping to fulfill His purposes in this hour. It is a role tailor-made for you and only you can fill that role. How do you find where you fit in missions? Let me suggest several things.

1. Discover your spiritual gifts

You can congratulate yourself – God only has gifted children and He has given every believer certain gifts. These gifts are for edifying and building up the body of Christ. You may have the gift of administration. If so, you could be used in volunteer work with a missions organization, or God may want to use you permanently in the administrative side of a missions ministry. If you have the gift of helps, you could invest your vacation time in going and doing all of the hands-on work that takes up so much of the time of missionaries and native pastors. If you have the gift of tongues, you should move into intercession in an even deeper way for the nations and unreached peoples of our world. So discover your spiritual gift and use it for God's purposes in this hour.

2. Discern your natural abilities

Natural abilities are not the same as spiritual gifts, although they usually complement each other. It is important that you utilize your natural abilities for the advance of the gospel. Has God given you the ability to sing? Use that talent in any opening God gives you, including nursing homes and rescue missions. Participating in ministries like these brings the smile of God on your life. Do you have ability as a mechanic? Believe me, you are needed in the Two-Thirds World and you can bring great blessing and help to many missionaries.

3. Define your circumstances

If you are careful as a steward and sacrificial, you will probably discover that you have at least some income that you may use at your discretion. Use it to promote the gospel around the world. And if obligations hinder you from going overseas, remember that your light can shine wherever you are and that there are plenty of cross-cultural opportunities for ministry right in your own home town.

A young man once said to me, 'I'm called to Germany.' Only half-teasing, I smiled and said, 'No, you're not.' 'What do you mean?' he retorted. 'My point is, you're not called to Germany, you're called to **Germans**. And before I encourage you to uproot your family and move to Germany, I'd like to know about your ministry right here in this city to those people whose primary language and cultural orientation is German.'

4. Discern the seasons of life
God may be calling you to hands-on missionary service in another season. If so, discern what season of life He has placed you and serve Him with joy in every season of life.

I want to reemphasize that I believe **every Christian** is called to missions, although we do not all have the cross-cultural gift of being missionaries. Perhaps the best advice is simply to start now with 'whatever your hand finds to do.' I have discovered something in missions. If you will simply let it be known that you truly care about God's purposes, about missionaries, about national pastors and works, about unreached peoples, and if you will take even faltering steps toward missions involvement, you will soon be deluged with opportunities. Then your greatest challenge will be to discern what assignments have been truly given to you by God.

God did not make a mistake when He called on you to represent Him in this hour of the church's history and at this pregnant, once in a lifetime moment. Don't fritter away your days in this thrilling era of opportunity. Get up! Do something and trust the Holy Spirit to guide your steps.

The Church's Finest Hour

The dark side of the history of missions is the tragedy of missed opportunities. At the end of World War II, General Douglas MacArthur pleaded with the American church to rush thousands of missionaries to a humbled, defeated Japan. Shintoism had failed them. Their 'god,' Hirohito, had just been 'de-deified.' It was a classic moment of opportunity for Christianity to walk into a colossal vacuum. Instead, the church hesitated. In the minds of many American Christians the Japanese were still the enemy. And while we stalled, Japan groped toward a new religion – shameless, often vicious materialism. Is there a consequence, other than spiritual, when missions opportunities are lost? You better believe it.

I am tired of hearing about 'closed doors' to the gospel. I agree with what Brother Andrew has said:

> 'There are no closed doors to the gospel – provided that, once you get inside, you don't care if you ever come out!'

And even if doors are closing, new windows of opportunity are opening all the time. The church must be poised to crawl rapidly through these seasonal open doors.

If ever there was a time to rise to the challenge and in the Spirit's power attempt great things for God, that time is now. This can be the church's finest hour.

When our sons were small, Naomi and I would tuck our little boys into bed by singing them a song that was anything but a lullaby. In fact, it sounded more like an anthem and a call to arms. But we wanted it to be the last thing that went into our sons' hearts and minds as they drifted to sleep.

Rise up, O men of God,
Have done with lesser things.
Give heart and soul and mind and strength,
To serve the King of Kings.
Rise up, O men of God,
The church for you doth wait.
Her strength unequal to her task,
Rise up and make her great.

Whoever you are reading this book, will you take the challenge to make this the church's finest hour? Will you pull out all the stops and throw your life into the gathering of today's bumper crop of spiritual harvest around the world?

Starting Now

How do you begin? Let me give you several steps you can take, starting as soon as you put this book down.

1. Give obediently

A greater heart for missions starts in the purse and the pocketbook. Why? Because Jesus said our hearts always follow our treasure.

> *'Do not store up for yourselves treasures on earth, where moth and rust destroy, and where thieves break in and steal. But store up for yourselves treasures in heaven, where moth and rust do not destroy, and where thieves do not break in and steal. For where your treasure is, there your heart will be also.'* (Matthew 6:19–21)

Give as you're prompted by God's Spirit to your church's missions program, individual missionaries, credible mission agencies, and ministries to the poor.

Treasures in heaven are the soundest investment on earth! Our checkbooks are not merely a record of our financial transactions, they are a diary of our priorities. They tell on us. They tell what is important to us. A businessman once asked me, 'David, how can I be more involved and have more of a heart for missions?' I said, 'Sir, the answer is simple and specific. Write out a check for $1,000 and earmark it for missions. Place it in the offering plate and I promise you, you will have more of a heart for missions!' Believe me, it just works that way. Where your treasure is, there your heart will be.

Notice the cause and effect. Where our treasure is (present tense), there our heart will be (future tense). Where our treasure is (cause), there our heart will be (effect). In other words, if you need a change of heart, redirect your assets. Put your money where your heart ought to be.

In the early 1950s, there was a precious, praying grandmother who lived in Florida. She faithfully prayed for missionaries and for the gospel's advance around the world. One day as she was praying the Lord gave her a vision and she saw the word '**Ceylon**.' Ceylon is today's Sri Lanka, just south of India. As she continued to pray she saw in her spirit a young man, perhaps in his late teens, sitting outside the gates of a Bible school in Ceylon. He was crying because he did not have the money to be admitted to the Bible school. After seeing this vision, this grandmother got up off her knees and called the mission director of her church. She said, 'You know I don't have much education and I don't know much about geography but somewhere in the world there must be a place called Ceylon. The Lord has shown me there is a young man who wishes to go to Bible school in Ceylon but he doesn't have the money to be admitted. I'm going to send the money to you,' she continued, 'and you send the money to him.' She did it. And as the money arrived in Ceylon there was in fact a young man sitting outside the gates of a Bible school crying. Compassionate officials had just turned him away saying, 'Son, we're sorry, but times are so difficult we simply cannot admit another student who cannot pay.' Not knowing what to do and only knowing that God had called him, he just sat there and wept – when the money for him arrived.

That is not the end of the story. That young man today is my personal friend. His name is Colton Wicknamaratne. Today he pastors the largest church in the nation of Sri Lanka. Just think. It all could have been aborted had it not been for the sensitivity of a child of God who gave obediently. I wonder how many Coltons there are today who are desperately praying that somebody will be God's channel for the answering of their desperate prayers.

In 1995 the Global Consultation on World Evangelization convened in Seoul, Korea. Our venue was the state-of-the-art Korean World Mission Center, valued at over 40 million US dollars. This magnificent center for world evangelization is the gift of one Korean Christian businessman. God wants to give many in His church enormous fiscal strength so that they might advance His purposes.

2. Pray globally

Years ago Ruth Graham was asked if she used a prayer book in her devotions. 'Yes,' she replied, 'the morning newspaper.' Every major event affects the gospel, either favorably or adversely. So pray over current events. Pray too for countries in a systematic way. I use Dick Eastman's *World Prayer Map* and Patrick Johnstone's *Operation World* as aids to global intercession. Don't forget to pray by name for missionaries and national workers, lifting their needs to God. Then pray specifically for unreached peoples. The *Global Prayer Digest* is excellent for this purpose. Youth With A Mission provides a terrific daily prayer journal for the nations and unreached peoples. Nothing connects you with the purposes of God more than catching the Spirit's intercession as He sweeps over the earth to accomplish God's agenda.

3. Love cross-culturally

If you can't go overseas, take heart. The world is coming to you! There are many ministries now that provide excellent avenues for caring involvement with international students. Thousands of tomorrow's foreign leaders are studying in schools in America and Britain right now. Most international students desperately want Western friends. You can be their link with the love of Christ. Thousands of students leave America and Britain disappointed. They had wanted to discover the truths of Christianity and friendship with the people of the nation. Too often they find neither.

Mhomar Khadafy fine-tuned his hatred for Americans while he was a student at an American college. The three men who led the attack on Pearl Harbor fine-tuned their hatred for Americans on campuses of American colleges. Let us not be guilty of the same.

Jesus stated that a sure sign of His soon return would be that *'nation will rise against nation'* (Matthew 24:7). The word Jesus uses is the Greek word *ethnos*. Jesus clearly prophesied that just prior to His return there would be much ethnic based conflict in the world. We in the church are to stand as a counter to this evil and display our oneness and unity in the body of Christ.

4. Work differently

However you acquire your necessary finances, your true

vocation as a Christian is to love God and to make Him loved, to know God and to make Him known.

> *'Whatever you do, work at it with all your heart, as working for the Lord, not for men.'* (Colossians 3:23)

Wherever you are you represent the Lord Jesus Christ and are part of the fabric of His Master Design. Every day Christians are spread out over the nations as the salt of the earth and the light of the world.

> *'Let your light shine before men, that they may see your good deeds and praise your Father in heaven.'*
> (Matthew 5:16)

5. Go personally

For many people, going out of town is not an option, much less going overseas. But we live in an increasingly mobile world. Technology has turned us into a global village. I'm told that at any given time there are some eight million Americans in other countries. If there is a potential of travel for you, there are several options.

To serve the Lord in another land or in an area here that needs your love, you don't have to be called to be a missionary. Perhaps you could invest your vacation in missions. Or consider missions trips sponsored by your church. Perhaps you work for a multi-national company. You could pray about an overseas transfer. You may have a skill that is needed in developing nations.

There are vast opportunities for short-term service, especially for young people. This is where much of the action is in missions expansion. Most missions organizations provide short-term opportunities ranging from a month to two years. Your church may be involved in a summer outreach. Take advantage of these great opportunities.

When you have personal hands-on missions involvement, even if it's only for a week or two, there's something like a missions serum that gets injected into your spiritual bloodstream. From then on you become a 'carrier' of missions enthusiasm and an advocate for world evangelization.

More than anything I have mentioned, however, is the need for a complete devotion to Jesus Christ. Shortly before David Livingstone died, he was offered a final opportunity to come back to Britain to the accolades that were certainly due him. He was asked, 'Why, Dr Livingstone, are you living in obscurity when your name is a household word in the civilized world? Why are you living here in poverty when your books are best sellers, both in Britain and the United States? Why are you fighting these tropical diseases when we have new medical treatments you could avail yourself of in Britain?' Livingstone replied that he had long ago made a promise, both to God and to the Africans he so dearly loved, that he would live and die in Africa. In fact, after his death in a posture of prayer in an African hut, before his body was returned to England for burial in highest honor at Westminster Abbey, as per his instructions, his heart was cut out and forever buried in African soil.

Livingstone wrote these words in his diary shortly before his death:

'My Jesus, my King, my life, my all – I again dedicate the entirety of my life unto Thee.'

What will it take to finish the job and get the gospel to every person and plant a church for every people group in our lifetime? A new generation must arise who will say from their hearts, 'My Jesus, my King, my life, my all – I again dedicate the entirety of my life to You.'

Chapter 8

Priesthood
The Glory of His Presence

Sweet strains of hymns sung in harmony drifted with the breezes through the gentle South Pacific air. Splashes of brilliant color covered the football field as thousands of happy Christians marched toward the platform in their native dresses and costumes. They came singing, waving branches, some with shouts of joy, all of them with thanksgiving. When each group reached the platform, large pouches were opened and poured out on a table, as coins from children and larger cash from adults swelled into a literal mound of currency. The churches of Fiji had gathered for their annual festival to bring their missions offerings to God.

As I watched this moving scene from the speaker's platform, I wept. God was being exalted by beautiful native peoples who only a generation earlier were far from Him. But thanks to God-honoring missionaries, not only had these thousands of Fijians found Christ, they were eager to honor Him and share Him with others.

I remembered the dying words of the sacrificial missionary, John Hunt, 'O let me pray for Fiji. O Lord, save Fiji!' My eyes were witnessing to a large degree the fulfillment of the prayer of this sacrificial missionary one hundred years earlier. A surge of gratitude raced through my heart as I witnessed first-hand the trans-generational faithfulness of God. What we pray today can break through the time barrier and reverberate in blessing for generations yet unborn.

Then I remembered the passionate cry of Francis Xavier as he stood on an island looking toward what seemed to him the impregnable hearts of China's millions. 'Rock, rock,' he cried, 'when will you open to my Savior?' Xavier might still pray that prayer today; but he would be encouraged that one of the largest, most powerful national churches on earth now exists in China!

Almost every nation on earth now has a verifiable church, although many must gather clandestinely. Every unreached people group has now been identified and cooperative efforts to reach them are progressing at record speed. Daily we move ever closer to the full realization of the Psalmist's missions-drenched prayer,

> 'May the nations be glad and sing for joy,
>   for you rule the peoples justly
>   and guide the nations of the earth.
> May the peoples praise you, O God;
>   may all the peoples praise you.'   (Psalm 67:4,5)

Let the Nations be Glad!

Certainly we should honor the faithful obedience of every missionary effort, both past and present. At the same time, we need to refocus much of our thinking about world evangelization. The Holy Spirit wants to shift our focus from merely **local** thinking to **global** thinking; from a **temporal** orientation to an **eternal** orientation.

Most of all, He wants to turn us from **man-centered** missions to **God-centered** missions.

Note the following missions challenges:

> 'People are perishing. The nations are starving, both physically and spiritually. We have a duty to get the gospel to the unreached. A basic humanitarian concern mandates that we do something for the destitute. We have so much. What about those who have so little? We are people of destiny. We must finish the task!'

I believe every word of the previous paragraph. In fact, I embrace every challenge with deep conviction. But, look at those challenges again. Where is God? Each of those statements is both true and legitimate. But is it the ultimate rationale for world evangelization?

Much of the missions enterprise has been centered around people – the physical and spiritual plight of humanity and the obligation of Christians to respond. In our missions preaching we have appealed to duty, we have cajoled with guilt, we have prodded with inspiration. I know, I've done it myself. But again, where is God?

John Piper has rightly observed,

> 'Missions is not the ultimate goal of the church. Worship is. Missions exists because worship doesn't. Worship is ultimate, not missions, because God is ultimate, not man. When this age is over, and the countless millions of the redeemed fall on their faces before the throne of God, missions will be no more. It is a temporary necessity. But worship abides forever. Worship, therefore, is the fuel and goal of missions.' [1]

Priesthood of All Believers – for Unbelievers

The biblical functions of a priest include offering accept-able worship and sacrifices to God and interceding for others. A great, recovered truth from the Reformation is that every Christian is to function as a priest;

> *'You have made them to be a kingdom and priests to serve our God ... '* (Revelation 5:10)

As priests, we have direct access to God. We need no mediator other than the one great mediator, Jesus Christ (see 1 Timothy 2:5).

Let's look briefly at the office of a priest. In his mediatorial role, he is to offer sacrifices in behalf of others. This was the role of priests throughout the Old Testament. It was a role that grew with time, as God progressively unveiled His plan to redeem all humanity. In early recorded history a man would offer the sacrifice of an innocent animal in behalf of himself and his immediate family. Later one sacrifice was sufficient to be offered for an entire tribe. Still later it was one annual sacrifice in behalf of the whole nation. Then, finally, when John saw Jesus, he pronounced, *'Look, the Lamb of God, who takes away the sin of the **world**!'* (John 1:29).

No more sacrifice for sin is needed. Jesus *'entered the Most Holy Place once for all by his own blood, having obtained eternal redemption'* (Hebrews 9:12). The sacrifice of sin has been paid. Now, we offer the sacrifice of thanksgiving and praise for the redemption that Christ purchased for us.

But what would be a fitting, God-honoring offering of gratitude for Christ's great sacrifice for sin on the cross? Paul gives us the astounding answer. He said, '[he had] *the priestly duty of proclaiming the gospel of God, so that the Gentiles* [i.e. the nations] *might become an offering acceptable to God, sanctified by the Holy Spirit.'* (Romans 15:16)

In other words, Paul was saying that the greatest gift of worship we could ever present to God would be to offer redeemed nations, that His blood has purchased, back to Him! And how does this happen? By proclaiming the gospel to the nations! Our first action as biblical priests is to offer acceptable worship; and the greatest oblation of worship to a worthy God would be to present back to Him His fallen, redeemed, restored creation.

Steve Hawthorne poignantly observes,

'Paul's passionate ambition to "preach the gospel" was based on the far more fundamental commission (or in his language, a "grace that was given") which he had received from God to "priest the gospel." ... Paul sees himself before God, serving the nations as if he were a priest, instructing and ushering them near to God, helping them bring the glory of their nation to God for his pleasure.'[2]

Our other role as priests is to intercede. In other words, we are to 'stand in the gap' for others. Having perfectly fulfilled His role as Redeemer, Jesus' high priestly role now is as our great Intercessor.

'*He is able to save completely those who come to God through him, because he always lives to intercede for them.'* (Hebrews 7:25)

Christ intercedes for us as **believers** before our heavenly Father. But, our prayers and intercession are to be made *'for everyone'* (1 Timothy 2:1). We are to intercede, standing in between people and the consequences of their sin. As faithful intercessors we petition God for mercy, asking that their sins would be covered by a gracious evangelistic outpouring and reception of the gospel.

Not only have we become children of God through faith in Christ, we have become priests to God, as well. We long for the gospel to reach every nation, every person. So, as faithful priests and intercessors, our hearts cry,

> *'Be exalted, O God, above the heavens;*
> *let your glory be over all the earth.'*   (Psalm 57:11).

And by faith we hear His response:

> *'I will be exalted among the nations,*
> *I will be exalted in the earth.'*   (Psalm 46:10)

Mary Versus Martha

We have tragically dichotomized what God has joined together. Too often we have pitted the 'activist evangelism types' against the 'mystic worship types.' We have appealed to the story of Mary and Martha, citing Jesus' accolades to Mary for sitting at His feet and His loving yet clear rebuke to Martha for placing service **for** Him as antecedent to simply being **with** Him. 'Don't be like Martha,' we sermonize.

I agree. However, it is equally dishonoring to Jesus when we do not allow worship to prod us to Christ-honoring action. Certainly we dare not attempt ministry without first experiencing His fellowship and presence. Yes, worship should change us. But change us for what?

We are changed and empowered in His presence in order that we may accomplish His purposes. Jesus' own life exhibits this beautiful rhythm of stealing away to commune with His Father then diving immediately into the turbulence of humanity's pain. Then, having poured Himself out to others in ministry, He would again retreat to the quiet place with His Father.

Paul understood this cause and effect of fellowship and ministry. In Philippians 3:10 he cries out,

> *'I want to know Christ and the power of his resurrection and the fellowship of sharing in his sufferings, becoming like him in his death.'*

Pretty intimate stuff. Then immediately he says he will *'press on to take hold of that for which Christ Jesus took hold of me'* (Philippians 3:12). Pretty activist stuff. Paul was saying, 'With the same level of tenacity with which Jesus caught me, I'm going to catch hold of what He had in mind when He saved me. I'm determined to discover what He wants out of me – and I'm determined to give it to Him.'

I readily admit this book is a call to action. I don't retreat from that for one second. But I would not want you to think I am merely championing a cause, even a cause as noble as world evangelization. What I am urging is that we so freshly fall in love with Jesus that what is precious to Him becomes precious to us, and what is priority for Him becomes priority for us. There can be no mistake about what is precious and priority for Him:

> *'The Son of Man came to seek and to save what was lost.'*
> (Luke 19:10)

Glory Evangelism

For the last several years in missions circles we have stressed **power evangelism**. There's even a chapter in this book devoted to the subject. This emphasis has been necessary in order to bring the entire evangelical community into conformity both with Scripture and the prevailing world view that embraces supernatural phenomena as a normal, not abnormal, part of life.

By and large, this has been accomplished, at least in the missions community. Most missions-active Christians today embrace the present-tense, powerful acts of God worldwide that are confirming the power of the gospel. But now a caution needs to be extended, particularly to those of us who might call ourselves charismatics.

The caution is this: Healings, deliverance and miracles ought to point somewhere. And where they should point is **directly to the cross of Jesus Christ!** Surely a genuine encounter with the living God will reorient our lives and dramatically alter our priorities. Yet we seem to espouse a sort of 'Pentecostal narcissism.' For the last several years I have blushed with embarrassment as I've watched too many of my fellow charismatics massage **their** egos, luxuriate in **their** creature comforts and infer that the ultimate purpose of God is **their** happiness and well-being. Where are all of our 'feel good' revivals taking us?

Are we as insensitive as the nine lepers who went their merry way once they were healed? I have no problem with thousands of Christians 'doing some serious carpet time.' But I have a major problem with those who stay light-headed once they get up from the carpet and continue living without a clue as to **His** honor, **His** glory and their role in fulfilling **His** purposes in the earth!

While embracing signs and wonders, it is time to move beyond **power evangelism** to **glory evangelism**. In any given situation among the nations, God may or may not demonstrate certain ones of His powerful acts. But He **always** desires to reveal His glory. He wants to be honored by the mosaic of every culture He Himself has created. It was this longing for God's glory to be manifested among all peoples that drove early Christians into missions.

> *'It was for the sake of the Name that they went out.'*
>
> (3 John 7)

They ached for **the fame of His name** among every nation!

Hawthorne writes:

> 'God desires the glory that he deserves ... He seeks to be recognized by all, and to be lovingly served by many from every people. God is worthy of such glory, but what is astounding to comprehend is that he actually takes joy in the glory that people can bring him ... The basic rationale for world evangelization is that God reveals his glory to all peoples so that he may receive glory from all creation.'[3]

Missions' Highest Motivation

People are eternally lost without Jesus Christ. Surely that should make us missions activists, but it is not our highest motivation. The needs of humanity are immense and desperate. Yes, we should identify with their suffering and seek to heal the open festering wounds of our world. Yet, though noble, this is not to be our highest motivation. Talk of 'discovering our destiny' may be the right motivation or it may be just more thinly veiled narcissism. If 'fulfilling our purpose' just means finally figuring out what my gifts are and getting a kick out of using them, we're carnal narcissists, no matter how much we may protest to the contrary. But if 'fulfilling our purpose' means throwing all of our energies, gifts and influence into extending His glory throughout the earth, then we're getting the point.

With Paul, our highest motivation should be to offer all peoples to God as trophies of His grace that He might receive the worth and honor that is due only to Him. It's no wonder that the new song of the redeemed from every tribe, language and people peals out with the loud declaration,

> *'Worthy is the Lamb, who was slain, to receive power and wealth and wisdom and strength and honor and glory and praise!'* (Revelation 5:12)

In this once in a lifetime bumper crop harvest, we need to focus on God's glory among every people, not just the size of the harvest. **Our service and love is not first to the harvest, it is to the *Lord of the harvest*!** We crave His honor in all the earth. Charles Wesley expressed it magnificently in his paean of praise, *O For a Thousand Tongues*:

> My gracious Master and my God
> Assist me to proclaim,
> To spread through all the earth abroad
> The honors of Thy Name!

References

1. John Piper, *Let the Nations Be Glad!* Grand Rapids, Mich.: Baker Book House, 1993, p. 11.

2. Steve Hawthorne, 'The Story of His Glory,' *Mission Frontiers Bulletin*, May–June 1993, p. 49.
3. *Ibid.*, p. 43.

Chapter 9

Purity
The Case for Salt and Light

*'I, the Lord, have called you in righteousness;
I will take hold of your hand. I will keep you
and will make you to be a covenant for the
people and a light for the Gentiles, to open eyes
that are blind, to free captives from prison and
to release from the dungeon those who sit in
darkness.'* (Isaiah 42:6–7)

What is the greatest detriment to the evangelization
of the world today? Is it a lack of finances? Is it a lack of
personnel? Is it a lack of cooperation? Is it the resistance
of obstinate governments? Is it the strength of Islam? Is it
secularism? What, more than any other factor, is prevent-
ing us from evangelizing the world?

You may be surprised at my answer. I lay the blame
for our failure not at the feet of Muslims, belligerent
governments or disinterested secularists. **The greatest
impediment to world evangelization today is the
carnality of the church!**

Someone has well remarked that the church has

survived through many centuries both the wrath of its enemies and the ineptitude of its members. Nevertheless, the ineptitude of those who name the name of Christ is by far a greater problem than the wrath of our enemies. In fact, Christianity seems to thrive in the soil of persecution. The fastest growing church in the world today is in China, yet the Chinese government has harassed, persecuted, imprisoned, and sometimes martyred Christians since communism came to power in the early 1950s. When Western missionaries were forced out of China, there were one million Christians. Today there may be as many as one hundred million believers in China, making it the nation in the world with the most Christians.

The growth of the gospel worldwide has been nothing less than astounding. According to the US Center for World Mission, the number of non-Christians per Great Commission Christians has dramatically shrunk within the last few decades. Look at this amazing trend.

1430 AD	1 out of every 100 people on earth were Bible believing Christians.
1790 AD	1 out of every 50
1940 AD	1 out of every 33
1960 AD	1 out of every 25
1970 AD	1 out of every 20
1980 AD	1 out of every 17
1989 AD	1 out of every 11
1993 AD	1 out of every 10 [1]

Where we get into trouble is when we assume that all who name the name of Christ are in fact truly Christian. This has sparked considerable discussion within the missions community. Are all of those who claim to be Christians to be labeled as such? While everyone agrees we should give special attention to the 10/40 Window where most of the unreached peoples reside, are we to forsake Europe simply because it is 'Christian'? I do not believe that Europe is 'post-Christian.' I believe the European continent, along with every other continent, is pre-Christian. No continent has yet come under the full lordship of Christ. Even seasons of great renewal and reformation were only preparatory to what God truly has in mind.

The day in which we live calls for radical commitment. Someone asked me recently, 'What are you?' I replied, 'I am a global, liberal, evangelical, charismatic radical!' By that I mean that the new kind of Christian God is raising up for the fulfilling of His purposes has a global perspective, a liberal heart (not to be confused with liberal theology or liberal politics), an evangelical theology, a charismatic experience, and a radical commitment to Jesus Christ!

Jesus said,

> *'You are the salt of the earth ... you are the light of the world.'* (Matthew 5:13, 14)

As such, He urges us to:

> *'... let your light shine before men, that they may see your good deeds and praise your Father in heaven.'*
> (Matthew 5:16)

Everywhere we look people and nations are in desperate need. We are called to be salt and light, but Jesus warns that we are not to lose our saltiness nor are we to allow our light to grow dim. Sin short-circuits God's purpose in our lives, destroying our saltiness and dimming our light.

What Kind of People?

I do not espouse the classical liberalism of Harry Emerson Fosdick. However, my heart leaps in agreement with the prayerful words of his magnificent hymn:

> God of grace and God of glory,
> On Thy people pour Thy power;
> Crown Thine ancient church's story,
> Bring her bud to glorious flower.
> Grant us wisdom, grant us courage,
> For the facing of this hour.
>
> Lo! the hosts of evil round us
> Scorn Thy Christ, assail His ways!
> Fears and doubts too long have bound us,
> Free our hearts to work and praise.
> Grant us wisdom, grant us courage,
> For the living of these days.
>
> Set our feet on lofty places;
> Gird our lives that they may be
> Armored with all Christ-like graces
> In the fight to set men free.
> Grant us wisdom, grant us courage,
> That we fail not man nor Thee.

In light of the impending Day of the Lord, Peter asks the piercing question,

> *'What kind of people ought you to be? You ought to live holy and godly lives as you look forward to the day of God and speed its coming.'* (2 Peter 3:11–12)

In the days in which we live, we are *'to live holy and godly lives.'* This is only possible as we draw upon the resources of the Holy Spirit. I love what the great missionary to the Muslim world, Samuel Zwemer, said:

'There is no more congenial soil in which to cultivate the fruit of the Spirit than near the Throne of Grace.'[2]

As we are in the presence of the Lord we

'...*are being transformed into his likeness with ever-increasing glory, which comes from the Lord, who is the Spirit.*'
(2 Corinthians 3:18)

Out of our fellowship with the Lord we then are thrust by Him into the world with all its needs. The world is not to dominate us, we are to dominate the world. The world is not to change our character, we're to change the character of the world. Elton Trueblood speaks pointedly to this important feature. 'Christ did not employ the concept of remnant, but used, instead, the utterly different idea of leaven,' Trueblood writes:

'Superficially, the two ideas are similar, since both refer to what is small, but they lead in opposite directions. A people trying to be a remnant, keeping itself pure and undefiled in the midst of a wicked world, may reveal a certain nobility of character, but it is radically different from the pattern taught by Christ. The wonder of leaven is that it is effective, not by keeping itself separate from the world, but rather by penetrating the world.'[3]

So how does this all shake down in modern life? It means that we as world Christians are not only focused on getting the gospel to the ends of the earth and establishing viable churches among all unreached peoples; it also means that we are allowing the Holy Spirit to daily transform us into the very image of Christ. We welcome the cultivation of His fruit and the release of His gifts. In very practical ways it means that:

1. World Christians are **faithful people**. We are faithful to our vows. We are faithful to our spouses. We are faithful to God. We are faithful to our church. We are faithful to our employers. We are faithful to show up at work. We are faithful to give an honest day's work. We are faithful to serve humanity in the name of Christ, serving in His name and as a gift to Him.

2. World Christians are **people of integrity**. There is no duplicity in our lives. We are who we say we are. The public persona and the private person are one and the same. Although we are not perfect, we hold up the ideal of the person of Jesus Christ and believe God's Word when He commands us,

    'Be holy, because I am holy.'   (1 Peter 1:16)

3. World Christians are **accountable people**. We get in small groups of accountability and allow the hard questions to be asked of us. I am deeply grateful for my friendship with Mike Downey, president of Global Missions Fellowship. We meet together as executives of two mission organizations to hold each other accountable in our personal lives. Each time we meet we ask each other the following questions.

    Since we last met...
    – Have you had a daily time with the Lord?
    – Have you been completely above reproach in all your financial dealings?

- Have you fulfilled the mandate of your calling?
- Have you been with a woman in a way that could be perceived as inappropriate?
- Have you sought out any explicit or pornographic material?
- How is your marriage?
- Have you just lied?

4. World Christians are **expectant people**. Peter said we are to live godly lives as we look for and hasten the coming of the Lord. We are to expect the return of Jesus Christ. We also, in some amazing way, hasten His return. God allows us the high dignity of participating in His very timetable by helping to fulfill the Great Commission. Jesus said,

    'And this gospel of the kingdom will be preached in the whole world as a testimony to all nations, and then the end will come.' (Matthew 24:14)

That means that we can actually hasten heaven's eschatology by seeing 'a church for every people and the gospel for every person.'

Since we will stand before a perfectly holy God, we must prepare our hearts in holiness. The very word **holiness** has fallen on hard times these days. Even some Christians mock the popular idea of 'holiness,' complete with its hypocrisy and holier-than-thou-ism.

But this is a distorted perception. Biblical holiness is light years removed from self-righteousness. Self-righteousness is just that, supposed goodness that is induced by one's own self. The biblical understanding of both righteousness and holiness is that they are produced and sustained by God alone. This is one of the unique features of the Christian faith. All other major religions are primarily an attempt on man's part to induce proper living and thus be accepted by some deity. But,

> *'... in the gospel a righteousness from God is revealed, a righteousness that is by faith from first to last, just as it is written: "The righteous will live by faith."'*
>
> (Romans 1:17)

The life of God is implanted in us when we are born again. This life is nurtured by obedience to the promptings of God's indwelling Spirit. Increased obedience produces increased sensitivity to sin. And this is the great need of our day. Our generation has become drugged and desensitized to sin and its effects.

What is the antidote? A megadose of genuine holiness. This is not merely for the mystics or the self-styled spiritual; it is for all who belong to Jesus Christ. There is a rather small segment of Christendom that is referred to as 'the holiness movement.' Actually, the entire body of Christ should be the holiness movement!

John Wesley transformed two nations by his call to holiness. He well understood the imperfections of his own life but he stated, 'I will preach holiness until I am holy. I will preach sanctification until I am sanctified.' We are not authorized to dilute the message or God's call to a holy life simply because we fall short of it.

I was appalled to hear the story of a professing Christian teenager recently. His girlfriend found out that she was pregnant. With no regard for the moral consequences, they determined to take what seemed to be the easiest course: she would have an abortion. As they were driving to the abortion clinic, the young man saw a stray dog with a broken leg. Immediately he stopped his car and, with a heart full of compassion for the lame animal, took the dog to the veterinarian, paying all expenses. Then he personally nursed the dog back to health.

Dear God, what has happened to us? This young man's conscience was highly sensitized to the plight of a stray dog but he was about to murder his own baby. It is past time for a moral revolution.

We do not know when death or Christ's coming will call us to account. But we do know that it will happen. We can prepare now by sensitizing our hearts. These words were written in the fly leaf of my father's Bible:

> 'This book will keep you from sin or sin will keep you from this book.'

There really is no middle ground and the time to face it is now.

The Bible speaks of a crown of righteousness which is reserved for those who so love the hope of Jesus' return that they have reordered their lives in view of His coming. This beautiful victor's garland is for those who have experienced the purifying effect of the imminent return of Christ.

When I was a boy my mother had a fool-proof way of correcting my bad behavior. All she had to do was to remind me, 'Your father is coming soon.' Believe me, it had a purifying effect! Just so, the prospect of the return of Christ at any moment has a sanctifying effect on the Christian's life. The blessed hope of Christ's imminent return is a purgative in our lives:

> *'Everyone who has this hope in him purifies himself, just as he is pure.'* (1 John 3:3)

The New Brand of Christian Leader

Who will be the next Billy Graham? Well, we all know that there will never be another Billy Graham, just as there has never been another Spurgeon or Moody. God always raises up a brand new expression of men and women to provide a standard for the rest of us. I do believe, however, that there will be at least one and possibly many great new international evangelists on the order of Billy Graham in the days ahead. I very much doubt that they will be from the Western world. I believe God has young people hidden in His quiver in the Two-Thirds World who will emerge in the 21st century as great international leaders of the body of Christ. One of them may be reading this book even now.

In this respect, David Yonggi Cho has been something of a John the Baptist. More and more in days ahead, Western church leaders will sit at the feet of men and women from the Two-Thirds World to be instructed by them in the ways of sacrifice, evangelism, worship, spiritual warfare and church growth.

I was moved to tears several years ago when I had been invited to the State House in Lusaka, Zambia, for a reception for national pastors hosted by the nation's president, Fredrick Chiluba. I stood in amazement watching Mr Chiluba, the head of state, personally and cordially pouring the tea and coffee, serving the pastors of his nation. How I thank God for this new breed of servant leader. The new leader God is raising up will have boldness without brashness, power without pride and anointing without arrogance.

In July of 1983 I was honored to attend the International Conference for Itinerant Evangelists in Amsterdam. From that meeting a biblical standard for evangelists emerged. It became something of a code of standards for Christian evangelists worldwide. Affirmation VIII declares,

'We acknowledge our obligation, as servants of God, to lead lives of holiness and moral purity, knowing that we exemplify Christ to the church and to the world.'

Commenting on this affirmation, Billy Graham wrote,

'Preaching is not the only way we declare the gospel of Christ. Our lives also should be witnesses to others of the reality of Christ. Those who have affected me most profoundly in my life have not necessarily been great or eloquent preachers, but men and women of God whose lives were marked by holiness and Christ-likeness. The gospel must be communicated not only by our lips but by our lives. This is a visual proof that the message we preach actually can change lives.

Our world today is looking for men and women with integrity, for communicators who back up their ministry with their lives. Our preaching emerges out of what we are. We are called to be a holy people – separated from the moral evils of the world.'[4]

It has often been stated that signs and wonders are the necessary ingredient for reaching unbelievers around the world. I fully concur that signs and wonders play a very important role. However, if this is somehow severed from lives of integrity, I am not sure that the world would get the message. It may be true that the primary need for the advance of the gospel in the Two-Thirds World is miracles. But the primary need for the advance of the gospel in the Western world is **integrity**.

A Wonderful Way to Spell Joy

When our lives are centered on Christ and on others, joy is the natural result. As little boys in Sunday School we used to sing,

'Jesus, others, and you.
What a wonderful way to spell JOY.'

Christ has called us to be His ambassadors, heaven's representatives, wherever we are. While giving great dignity to our lives, this should in no way make us arrogant or produce a superior attitude. My culture, compared to any other culture, is superior only insofar as the gospel has touched and transformed it. Missionaries are not superior people. All people are of equal worth to God. Nor do missionaries necessarily come from a superior culture. But they **do** proclaim a superior message and a superior way of life through Jesus Christ.

Some years ago I was talking to a businessman seated next to me on a plane. In the course of our conversation, he asked me, 'What do you do?' I responded, 'I'm an ambassador.' Surprised, he inquired further. 'What country do you represent? The United States?' I replied, 'No, I represent a kingdom far more powerful than the United States. I represent the kingdom of God!'

So do you, whether you're in your hometown or half a world away.

'We are therefore Christ's ambassadors, as though God were making his appeal through us. We implore you on Christ's behalf: Be reconciled to God.'

(2 Corinthians 5:20)

How wonderful it is to live for the glory of God by honoring His Son, the Lord Jesus, and how liberating it is to be free from a self-centered life! I do not know if the author of this poem was a Christian. However, I do know that he caught the essence of the heart of Jesus and found a wonderful way to live.

Is true freedom but to break
Fetters for our own dear sake,
And, with leathern hearts, forget
That we owe mankind a debt?
No! True freedom is to share
All the chains our brothers wear,
And, with heart and hand, to be
Earnest to make others free!
They are slaves who fear to speak
For the fallen and the weak;
They are slaves who will not choose
Hatred, scoffing and abuse,
Rather than in silence shrink
From the truths they needs must think;
They are slaves who dare not be
In the right with two or three.[5]

                                                    Lowell

Faithful Unto Death

In the few years remaining before AD 2000, most people
see a mixed bag of unprecedented opportunities coupled
with the potential for unprecedented clashes of religions
and ideologies. One pessimistic analyst, when asked to
predict the next few years, replied simply, 'Blood.' In
1995 some 157,000 people laid down their lives for the
testimony of Jesus.[6] There seems to be no possibility of
penetrating the Muslim world without significant
numbers of Christian martyrs.[7]

Throughout Christian history, churches have held a
theology of martyrdom. In fact, the very term is derived
from the Greek word for 'witnesses,' *martures*. David
Barrett notes,

'Martyrdom has been a standard accompaniment of Christian mission because Christians inevitably arouse hostilities, and they pay the price.'[8]

Martyrdom most often takes place in areas torn by civil strife and in the Islamic world. One believer who paid the ultimate price of devotion was Mehdi Dibaj, an Iranian Pentecostal leader, who was murdered in the summer of 1994. From prison, he wrote,

'I have always envied those Christians who all through church history were martyred for Christ Jesus our Lord. What a privilege to live for our Lord and to die for Him as well.'[9]

The Bible describes men and women like Pastor Dibaj as those *'of whom the world was not worthy'* (Hebrews 11:38 NKJV). By the strength of their unyielding love for Jesus, they have become a force to be reckoned with, a potent force in the earth.

It appears that every major religion is becoming more militant. A revived Islam is once again aggressively militant in many quarters. Bored with white magic, the occult has turned brutal. Probably because of the dramatic growth of the church in India in this decade, even Hindus, known historically as pacifists, are now often confrontational. The religion of secular humanism wages its propaganda war in theaters, courtrooms, classrooms, and legislatures, often winning. Many Christians are choosing to fight through acts of non-violent resistance.

It is indeed true that biblical Christianity is becoming more militant. But our militancy is of a different order. Our war is not with people; it is with demonic spirits who hold people captive. People who oppose Christianity are not the enemy. They are **victims** of the enemy. The bitter, almost perennially adversarial tone of many Christians and churches should be of grave concern to Christians who truly desire success in reaching people with the gospel. Our aggression is to be against Satan, not against the people who oppose us.

But aggressive we should be, if we remember that our battle is not with flesh and blood. Jesus said,

> *'From the days of John the Baptist until now, the kingdom of heaven has been forcefully advancing, and forceful men lay hold of it.'*   (Matthew 11:12)

All Christian advance is forceful advance. Some existing kingdom has to be displaced to plant the kingdom of God. This requires warfare – spiritual warfare. And, in most areas, it also requires demonstrations of God's power.

Our weapons are entirely different from those employed by other armies. And no effective counter has yet been found to our weapons! Bombs can be countered with bombs. Rhetoric can be countered with rhetoric. Hate can be countered with hate. But aggressive love – how do you counter that?

The International Christian army, equipped with 'God's power to demonstrate God's love,' is forcefully advancing worldwide. Africa, south of the Sahara, will be fifty percent Christian by the turn of the century. Evangelicals in Latin America (most of whom are Pentecostals and charismatics) are experiencing staggering growth. Even amid tragic scandals, America's charismatic churches continue to grow. Singapore, Korea, Thailand, and China have become hot points of the outpouring of the Holy Spirit in Asia. The Gospel is advancing in the island nations. And 'post-Christian' Western Europe is now experiencing isolated brush fires of revival that could become a continental flame.

But for the flames of revival to spread, for the purposes of God to be enacted, we must be salt and light. When the great American evangelist of the last century, J. Wilbur Chapman, was in London, he had an opportunity to meet General William Booth, who at that time was past eighty years of age. Dr Chapman listened reverently as the old General spoke of the trials, the conflicts and victories.

The American evangelist then asked the General if he would disclose his secret for success. Dr Chapman said,

> 'He hesitated for a second ... and I saw the tears come into his eyes and steal down his cheeks, and then he said, "I will tell you the secret. God has had all there was of me. There have been men with greater brains than I, men with greater opportunities; but from the day I got the poor of London on my heart, and a vision of what Jesus Christ could do with the poor of London, I made up my mind that God would have all of William Booth there was. And if there is anything of power in the Salvation Army today, it is because God has had all the adoration of my heart, all the power of my will, and all the influence of my life."' [10]

Will you, by the power of the Holy Spirit, raise a standard of integrity so that the world may know there is a God who transforms lives? Will you allow the light of Jesus to permeate through your personality so that men and women will be pointed to Him? God only knows the impact that could occur when you lay before Him all the adoration of your heart, all the power of your will, and all the influence of your life.

References

1. Sources: Lausanne Statistics Task Force and *Mission Frontiers*, US Center for World Mission, January/February 1994.
2. Samuel Zwemer, *Taking Hold of God, Studies on the Nature, Need and Power of Prayer*, London: Marshall, Morgan & Scott, n.d.
3. Elton Trueblood, *The Validity of the Christian Mission*, New York: Harper & Row, 1972, p. 7.
4. Billy Graham, *A Biblical Standard for Evangelists*, Minneapolis, Minn., Worldwide Publications, 1983, p. 73.
5. G.F. Main, *A Book of Daily Readings*, London: Collins, 1966, p. 86.
6. David Barrett, 'Annual Statistical Table on Global Mission: 1995,' *International Bulletin for Missionary Research*, January 1995, p. 25.
7. Kim A. Lawton, 'Killed in the Line of Duty,' *Charisma*, October, 1995, p. 59.
8. *Ibid.*, p. 56.
9. *Ibid.*, p. 59.
10. Paul Lee Tan, *Encyclopedia of 7700 Illustrations*, Rockville, Md.: Assurance Books, 1977, p. 1367.

Chapter 10

Passion
Loving Dangerously

I'm not even a British subject but I still had a lump in my throat.

Watching by television as the Union Jack was lowered for the final time over the strategic city of Hong Kong, I was reminded again of two realities. First, monumental changes are afoot in our world. Second, opportunities are fleeting.

I prayed and wondered what all this might mean for Christian believers in China. I've met with some of them. We in the West stand amazed at their courage and growth in the fertile soil of persecution. Every democratic instinct in me wants liberty for my brothers and sisters there. Yet I couldn't help but wonder if the one thing that could kill revival in China's churches might be Westernization. Years ago the late David Watson, a major leader in Britain's church renewal, suggested that Western Christianity probably would be too sapped of vitality to be a major player at the dawning of the twenty-first century.

I remembered the story of a Chinese teenager

imprisoned just last year for her testimony. Because she would not recant her faith for Jesus, she was placed for several months in solitary confinement. Finally a friend was allowed to see her. The friend whispered to the young prisoner to take heart because she knew that many Christians around the world were praying for believers in China. The young girl's response is instructive for us. 'Ask them to keep praying,' our sister told her. 'But please ask them not to pray for a lessening of persecution! Because when we're persecuted, we know His presence in a much greater way and we grow faster when persecution is more pronounced.'

That kind of theology is foreign to most of us in Western nations. But we need to listen again to our sister's request. We should certainly pray for our brothers and sisters in China and in other restrictive nations. We should ask the Holy Spirit to open the doors for a clear proclamation of the gospel and open hearts to receive it. And, even if it goes against our free world sensitivities, we should ask God to engineer the events of China and every nation to bring the greatest leverage for the growth of the church and the highest honor for the name of the Lord.

Love's Source

Even after suffering numerous injustices for the name of Jesus, Paul said, *'Christ's love compels us'* (2 Corinthians 5:14). That is what keeps us going, even when all other sources go dry. Even faith is fueled by love (see Galatians 5:6). How, then, is love itself fortified? The Bible says that

> *'God has poured out his love into our hearts by the Holy Spirit, whom he has given us.'* (Romans 5:5)

As noted missionary Elisabeth Elliot has said,

> 'The love of Christ constrains us. There is no other motivation for missionary service that is going to survive the blows of even the first year. You do it for Him.' [1]

A passion for Jesus and His global and eternal purposes must consume us.

I'm convinced there comes a point in every Christian's life when he or she makes some crucial life choices. Either you fall victim to the spirit of the age and embrace the cult of self or you live on a higher plane. The godly Francis Xavier challenged the apathetic European students of his day to 'give up their small ambitions and come and preach the gospel of Christ.' That same challenge echoes clearly today, except the opportunities are infinitely greater. Ralph Winter reminds us:

> 'There is no place on earth you cannot go in a few hours ... We must keep our goals clearly in mind and not worry too much about the details. We need not suppose that everything depends on us, but we must understand that God is asking everything of us. That, in turn, is the same as saying that He wants to touch our tongues with a live coal from the altar. It means He wants our love for all the world to reflect the genuineness and compassion of His love for all the world, which has already profoundly benefitted us. Paul explained his motivation when he said, *"Christ died for all that those who live might no longer live for themselves but for Him who died and rose again on their behalf."* (2 Corinthians 5:15).' [2]

So, what about you? Which will it be? Are you going to live to please yourself or to bring international acclaim to His name? Nobody's twisting your arm. The choice is entirely yours. But, remember this: **What you choose really does matter, both for your future and the future of our world, and you will give an account for your choice.**

Jesus Movement II

It is my deep conviction that a great international sweep of God's Spirit among young people is just around the corner. Just this year I stood in awe of God's hand as I watched 7,000 Indian young people answer my call to give their lives to preach the gospel and plant churches in northern India. Two years ago I saw 70,000 Korean college students stand in a drenching rain to offer their lives to Christ for His service in the 10/40 window.

Looking out on a sea of faces a few years ago in Thailand, I wept and praised God as I realized that almost everyone in the crowd of 11,000 where I was ministering was a young person in his teens or twenties. Even more remarkable was the fact that almost all were first generation Christians! These beautiful young people represented the first generation in Thailand's long history to break free in significant numbers from the ancient grip of Buddhism.

One girl whose face radiated the joy of Jesus told me her incredible story.

'I was raised in the red light district of Bangkok,' she told me. 'I wasn't there through any wish of my own; my parents had placed me there for money when I was a little girl.

'One day a preacher came to my room and put down money for me,' she continued. 'But he didn't buy me to use me for immoral purposes. He purchased me and took me home with him. He treated me as one of his own children. His family fed me, clothed me and shared the love of Jesus with me.'

With tears and a big smile she told me, 'Sir, I know what it means to be redeemed!' God has not overlooked Generation *X*. This precious generation, so battered and victimized by the sins of adults, will be raised up by God to seize this once in a lifetime harvest of humanity.

Last summer, thousands of American young people fanned out across the nations through Teen Mania and similar ministries. Teen Mania reported over 120,000 people who prayed to receive Christ through the witness of these young people. And, Jesus confirmed that He is alive in many thrilling ways. In Hong Kong, elderly people who had rejected the gospel throughout their lives, melted by the love of these teenagers, opened their hearts to Christ. In India, a tribe said they had been waiting 80 years for this good news. They began dancing for joy and the entire village had a party to celebrate the coming of the gospel. In Venezuela, a group of teenagers prayed for a man who had no eye. As they prayed, they watched the eye form in the socket and perfect vision come to the man.[3]

That's a demonstration of Christ's power that village will never forget. Nor will those teenagers. After seeing a miracle like that, they could attend 'Atheist University' and take courses from Professor Ima Skeptic and it wouldn't faze them!

God calls people of every age into His service but He always has His eye on the young generation. He has always been pleased to use young people. Perhaps it's because they don't know what the parameters are; they don't know what 'can't be done,' so they just go do it! The venom of unbelief has not yet poisoned their spiritual bloodstream.

Young people have always been in the forefront of the world missions march of the church. In the first era of missionary advance, God sent William Carey, not yet thirty, to forge the modern missions era. I remember standing in Nottingham where he preached his great sermon, urging his listeners to 'expect great things from God and attempt great things for God.' As I read the commemorative plaque, I thanked God that a new generation of His young firebrands from many nations are even now in the wings. I want to spend the rest of my life finding them, encouraging them and strengthening their hands.

Beware of the Counter-Attack

Some of the young people serving Christ today are among the greatest Christians in the world. The following story is well known throughout Peru and documented by believers there.

> Just a few years ago the so-called 'Shining Path' terrorists commandeered a Peruvian school high in the Andes mountains. Barging into a class of twelve-year-olds, they ordered every Christian student to stand. Immediately a young girl sprang to her feet. 'Renounce your faith in Jesus,' they ordered her, 'or we will beat you up.'
>
> 'I could never do that,' the girl responded. 'I love Jesus with all my heart.'
>
> The terrorists jerked her from her row, hauled her to the front and brutally beat her in front of her traumatized friends and teacher. Then they demanded, 'Now you must renounce your belief in Jesus or we will kill you.'

The girl replied, 'I've told you that I love Jesus Christ. It would be an honor to die for Him. I will never deny Him.'

With that, the shots rang out as the lifeless body of this young Christian martyr sunk to the floor. The teacher and students sat in shock and disbelief. Then, from the back of the room, one young boy began to chant, *'Cristo vive, Cristo vive, Cristo vive!'* Soon other courageous students stood and joined the chorus. Finally, the entire class was shouting back at the communist killers, 'Jesus is alive!' The terrorists were so shamed that they left the village and never returned.

This precious young girl, who offered Jesus the last full measure of her devotion, has now joined heaven's stadium of witnesses that are cheering us on.

> *'Therefore, since we are surrounded by such a great cloud of witnesses, let us throw off everything that hinders and the sin that so easily entangles, and let us run with perseverance the race marked out for us. Let us fix our eyes on Jesus, the author and perfecter of our faith . . .'*
>
> (Hebrews 12:1, 2)

We must not allow the overt persecution of antagonists, the well-intentioned tugs away from the harvest fields by Christians or the apathy of the carnal to deter us. Ross Paterson warns,

> 'There may be an active culture within the Church working against "praying, giving and going" for missions. Some leaders are threatened by the thought that their people or finances or prayer power might

be given to something which will not be measurable within the local church.' [4]

Whether we battle 'fightings from without or fears from within' we must stay committed to Christ and His purposes in our generation.

'Take This Position'

Far too many Christians are 'couch-potatoing' their way through life, either ignorant of or indifferent to God's glory in the earth and His purposes for our time. Suddenly they realize that the sand has sifted through the hourglass. They're out of time, out of touch, and, if they do go to heaven, they will go there out of treasure. They will have accomplished the sum total of nothing of eternal value.

I'm calling you today to a higher life. And I'm asking God to use this book to jolt thousands out of apathy and allow them to seize our once in a lifetime opportunity.

In preparation and research for this book, I went to the library of the venerable Yale Divinity School in New Haven, Connecticut. There I studied the original papers of a great missionary statesman of another era, John R. Mott. In 1900 Mott wrote a passionate plea to Christian young people titled, *The Evangelization of the World in This Generation*. Before its publication, however, he sent manuscript copies to selected individuals asking for their comments and suggestions. One of those manuscripts went to Hudson Taylor, the great missionary and founder of the China Inland Mission.

Now, ninety-six years later, I was holding in my hands the original letter from Hudson Taylor to John R. Mott. As I held Taylor's letter, I felt a glorious link with these two giants of an earlier day. I wondered what Taylor would think of the developments in China today and her virile church (much of which traces its roots back to his work). I mused how John R. Mott, the prime mover of student missions in his day, would rejoice to see an Urbana missions conference with 20,000 students or Youth With a Mission's thousands of passionate young people serving Christ around the world. Then I remembered that they do, in fact, see it all. They too are in that 'great cloud of witnesses.'

Looking again at Hudson Taylor's letter I read,

'The evangelization of the world depends on the full surrender of every Christian both at home and abroad, so that the Holy Spirit may be unhindered. Appeal to every reader to unhesitatingly take this position.'

Taylor's appeal to Mott's readers I am now making to you. Fully surrender your life to Jesus Christ. Let Him take the offering up of your precious life and use you for His purposes in ways beyond your highest hopes and dreams. When you are fully surrendered, then the Holy Spirit is unhindered and your life shifts from the realm called **natural** to the realm called **supernatural**. I call on you now to 'unhesitatingly take this position' of full surrender at the feet of Jesus.

Living for What Matters

In the late 1940s an American newspaper reporter was stationed in the city of Shanghai, China. He watched from the balcony of his hotel one horrific night as Mao tse Tung and troops loyal to Mao pillaged the city and burned much of it to the ground. The reporter watched as much as his stomach would allow. Finally he walked back into his room, sat at a little desk and wrote these words,

> 'Tonight Shanghai is burning, and I am dying too.
> But there's no death so real as the death inside of you.
> Some men die by shrapnel and some go down in flames,
> But most men die inch by inch, playing little games.'

Whatever else you may do, don't die inch by inch, playing little games. Live for what matters. And what matters is the exaltation of the Son of God to the ends of the earth.

References

1. David Shibley, ed., *Challenging Quotes for World Changers*, Green Forest, Ark.: New Leaf Press, 1995.
2. Ralph Winter, *Thy Kingdom Come*, Pasadena, Calif., New Leaf Press, 1995, p. 29.
3. Teen Mania, *Summer '97 Ministry Reports*.
4. Ross Paterson, *Explaining Mission*, Tonbridge, Kent: Sovereign World Ltd, 1994, p. 52.

Afterword

I woke up quite early this morning. It's a solemn day for much of the world, quite an ironic day to finish a book about fleeting opportunities. With literally billions of others this morning, I watched the funeral for Princess Diana.

Compounding the world's loss, Mother Teresa died yesterday. Much could be said about the contrast of lifestyles and loyalties between these two remarkable women. But this much they shared in common: both touched the lives of millions with genuine compassion. Both will be sorely missed by a generation where empathy is in high demand and short supply.

It's tempting to sermonize concerning the complexities of Princess Diana's tortured life. But for the purposes of this book there is one perspicuous lesson that must not escape us: **Even for the privileged, life is always tenuous and often very short**. The two backseat passengers on that fatal night, Princess Diana and Mr Fayad, had financial assets soaring beyond what most people can fathom. Yet their wealth could not purchase for them one more day. For the Princess of Wales, and for you and me, there is a scheduled appointment with eternity.

The Bible pointedly reminds us that we do not have the promise of tomorrow. If you have not made your peace with God through faith in His Son, for you,

> '…now is the time of God's favor, now is the day of salvation.'   (2 Corinthians 6:2)

Most people who read this book, however, already know Jesus Christ. Yet, having made life's most crucial choice, time for us should be even more precious. The promise of heaven is far more sure than the promise of long life. Not only that, the fact that there is a colossal global harvest **today** in no way ensures that it will be there tomorrow. Harvest is seasonal and short.

How then should we live? How do we seize today's bountiful, brief opportunities? I discussed this the other day with my friend and accountability partner, Mike Downey. Mike observed that, to seize today's opportunities, we must position our lives in three areas.

First, we must have **a passion for God**. Not first a passion for the harvest. Not a passion for 'the ministry.' Not even first a passion for people. A passion for God. His honor, in our hearts and throughout the earth, must be our highest desire.

Then we must make **a vow of integrity**. Paul lamented, *'God's name is blasphemed among the Gentiles because of you'* (Romans 2:24). He could have been talking about this generation of Christians. God have mercy on us and heal our backslidings. May we strive to keep our consciences clear before God and man (see Acts 24:16).

Finally, we must commit to **intentional involvement** in seizing today's opportunities. This plays out in clear, measurable ways: how we use our time, how we utilize our talents and where we put our money.

I discovered something this week in my Bible study I had never seen previously. I had long been very familiar with James's injunction,

> *'Anyone who knows the good he ought to do and doesn't do it, sins.'* (James 4:17)

In Sunday school as a little boy I learned that these were 'sins of omission,' and just as surely displeasing to God as 'sins of commission.' What I had never realized though was the context of that verse. James had just warned against arrogantly pronouncing that 'we'll do some long-term planning and then we'll go into our target city and make some real money' (my paraphrase). James cautioned that we ought to say, 'If it is the Lord's will, we will do this or that.' So far, so good.

But then I'm smacked with this conclusion statement. **Therefore** (that's what I hadn't seen earlier). **Therefore**, in light of the fact that the best laid plans of men can and do evaporate ... **Therefore**, since our life is no sturdier or longer than a mist ... **Therefore**, *'anyone who knows the good he ought to do and doesn't do it, sins!'*

The message is unmistakable. Has God told you to do something? Are you aware of 'something good you ought to do'? Then why are you sitting on it, as if you had the assurance of tomorrow? Get up and do it! Now! If you don't, you are blatantly sinning because you are presuming on a future that is not necessarily yours. The one moment ... the **one moment** you can really 'claim,' is this one.

> '**Once** to every man and nation comes **the moment** to decide.'

That pivotal, *kairos* moment for you – is now. So now, for

God's sake (and I mean that in the most reverential way), get up, seize opportunity and do exploits for the honor of His name.

If you have enjoyed this book and would like to help us to send a copy of it and many other titles to needy pastors in the **Third World**, please write for further information or send your gift to:

**Sovereign World Trust
PO Box 777, Tonbridge
Kent TN11 0ZS
United Kingdom**

or to the **'Sovereign World'** distributor in your country.